PRAISE ~~FOR~~

STRATEGIC IMPACT

"*Strategic Impact* is chock-full of useful tools and tips a leader from any size organization can apply to effectively conduct strategic planning. Dr. Poore draws on her many years of experience to provide practical tips for preparing for and conducting strategic planning sessions— including virtual ones. Her approach brings in the best thinking from renowned strategic thinkers and from the fields of appreciative inquiry, organizational development, and change management. A very useful and practical guide."

—JIM STOCKMAL, Association for Strategic Planning past president

"It's not enough to have a driving passion for a nonprofit mission. In order to achieve an organization's vision and values, it takes a concentrated approach. In *Strategic Impact*, Dr. Poore has created a structure that champions the process of thinking forward. Leading with intent along with a confident direction helps nonprofits build partnerships that achieve their mission. *Strategic Impact* gets to the heart of this journey in a manageable and achievable manner."

—JULIA C. PATRICK, CEO, American Nonprofit Academy

"*Strategic Impact* is on the mark. Dr. Carol Poore is knowledgeable about this topic and has shared her thoughts as a contributing member of *Phoenix Business Journal*'s Leadership Trust."

—RAY SCHEY, Market President and Publisher, *Phoenix Business Journal*

"All too often, strategic planning is an esoteric, academic exercise that rarely has a big impact. Dr. Carol Poore has done an excellent job of leveraging her experience in distilling the planning and execution of strategy into easy-to-understand steps. Her book is a roadmap into how to make an actionable plan and combine it with excellent tracking and communications to achieve great results."

—TED JACKSON, Co-founder and Managing Partner, ClearPoint Strategy

"In *Strategic Impact*, Dr. Carol Poore introduces an innovative strategic planning framework that will allow any leader to transform what is often a dreaded obligation (that usually turns into lengthy days of discussion, more frustrating than productive) into a vital and unifying leadership-team experience crucial to the organization's long-term success."

—SHARON LECHTER, CGMA, CEO of Pay Your Family First, author of *Think and Grow Rich for Women*, co-author of *Rich Dad, Poor Dad* and 14 other books in the Rich Dad series, and *Outwitting the Devil, Three Feet from Gold*, and *Success and Something Greater*

"As a leader, you'll want to keep *Strategic Impact* on your bookshelf of go-to books after you've read it cover to cover! This is a comprehensive and yet uncluttered book that will indelibly reinforce what you already know, remind you of things you have forgotten, and inspire you with fresh new tools, techniques, and approaches to make the strategic planning process an impactful and vital cultural cornerstone in your organization."

—DEBORAH BATEMAN, Vice Chairman of the Board of Directors, National Bank of Arizona, bank executive, and founder of Risk Blossoming Mentorship

STRATEGIC
IMPACT

A LEADER'S THREE-STEP
FRAMEWORK FOR
THE CUSTOMIZED
VITAL STRATEGIC PLAN

STRATEGIC
IMPACT

CAROL A. POORE, PH.D.

FC

FAST
COMPANY
Press

Fast Company Press
New York, New York
www.fastcompanypress.com

Distributed by River Grove Books

Design and composition by Greenleaf Book Group
Cover design by Greenleaf Book Group
© Miloje/Shutterstock Images
Illustrations by Justin Poore.
Copyright © 2020 by Justin Poore. All rights reserved.

Publisher's Cataloging-in-Publication data is available.

Paperback ISBN: 978-1-63299-316-8

Hardcover ISBN: 978-1-63299-318-2

eBook ISBN: 978-1-63299-317-5

First Edition

To my precious sons, Nathan and Justin—
May every chapter of your lives result in
Strategic Impact.

———

To my strategic planning colleagues around
the world, including corporate executives,
consultants, business owners, nonprofit and
community leaders, and all who are charged with
developing their organization's strategic
planning program—may your work result in
Strategic Impact.

vital (adjective)

Absolutely necessary or important; essential.
Full of energy; lively.
Life changing.

CONTENTS

This book includes a strategic planning bibliography featuring published strategic planning research, books, and articles spanning more than a hundred years. Visit www.VitalStrategicPlan.com for this reference resource. Visit www.CarolPoore.com for Vital Strategic Plan tools and techniques. These resources will be continually updated over time.

PREFACE

TODAY, LEADERS NEED A QUICK, EASY, and reliable strategic planning model that will lead to a meaningful leadership experience. They also need a clear, vital strategic plan that gets implemented. They don't have time to read complicated textbooks. They need an easy-to-understand approach, as well as tools, templates, and techniques they can use quickly to customize a strategic planning program that fits their unique organization.

I believe that *vital* strategic planning is a leadership experience that can be divided into three parts: your life-changing workshop, your compelling written plan, and your goal-tracking and communication system. For that reason I've created a three-part framework that will help you simplify the planning process while saving time and brainpower, so that you and your organization's leaders can focus on what's important:

- shaping an exceptional workshop without spending an exorbitant amount on consulting fees;

- customizing and communicating an engaging written plan, which can be further digitized and embellished in social media through storytelling; and

- tracking and communicating strategic goal progress.

Also, I share practical ways to incorporate virtual strategic planning into your program. Virtual planning helped mitigate the impact of chaos and mandatory social distancing required during the unprecedented COVID-19 global pandemic of 2020—considered by some as a disaster that defines our generation. The last global pandemic occurred in 1918 with the H1N1 influenza virus and was the deadliest pandemic of the twentieth century. Computer technology and the internet were nonexistent.

COVID-19 required emergency measures in the form of social distancing or sheltering at home to slow the devastating spread. Practically overnight, COVID-19, a virus with a mortality rate ten times that of seasonal flu, created an unprecedented culture of people working from home.

Across the world, as many lost jobs in sectors such as hospitality and the food and beverage business, others worked from home. Employees learned how to stay connected through virtual meetings, social media, and online technology. Courses were taught, church services were held, and meetings were convened online. Resources were shared through social media. Universities quickly pivoted from traditional classrooms to providing online classes through Zoom and other technologies.

Virtual meeting technology undoubtedly will continue to evolve as a result of the COVID-19 global pandemic. Through *Strategic Impact* I offer novel approaches to virtual strategic planning, including global panels, virtual discussions, war rooms, and "big rooms" for emergency strategy shaping, where employees can gather physically as well as remotely to address urgent situations requiring strategy and execution.

Unlike other strategic planning books, *Strategic Impact* declutters the process into a three-part framework or formula: the Strategic Planning Workshop (the shared leadership experience), the Written Strategic Plan (the shared story of strategic intent, shared digitally and with social media as well as in traditional print formats), and the System for Tracking and Communicating Results (the shared goal outcomes, or strategic impact).

Strategic Impact is a no-nonsense strategic planning how-to resource. The framework is time-tested and delivers results. You'll find client-approved strategic planning tools, tips, and techniques that can be used in hundreds of settings including corporate, nonprofit, trade association, small business, and start-ups. You can customize my vital workshop, written plan, and tracking templates, as well as select from a variety of tools and techniques to enhance your strategic planning program.

Strategic Impact will be especially helpful to the more than 98 percent of all US and worldwide businesses considered as "small"—up to twenty employees, according to the Small Business & Entrepreneurship Council.[1] Most of these organizations are unable to hire expensive consultants. Some are in dire financial stress where a strategic plan was needed yesterday.

Vital strategic plans are shaped by an organization's vital leaders, through a vital process. You are creating a vital leadership experience leading to your organization's future. Equally as important, you're shaping the destiny of many lives impacted by your organization.

I offer you a life-changing, legacy-shaping strategic planning experience that gets implemented and delivers results. Let's get started!

—Carol A. Poore, Ph.D., MBA
President, Poore & Associates Strategic Planning
Phoenix, Arizona
January 5, 2021

STRATEGIC PLANNING AS A LIFE-CHANGING LEADERSHIP EXPERIENCE

I DEVELOPED MY STRATEGIC PLANNING MUSCLE as a senior analyst at Salt River Project in Arizona, one of the largest public power and water companies in the United States—and where I saw experts spend their entire careers building thirty-year water resource plans. Few businesses present the unique dichotomy of straddling both long- and short-term planning perspectives.

As the Phoenix metro area was predicted to more than double in size within three decades, the organization needed to forecast an adequate supply of water and power to meet long-term demand. Also, the utility needed to be nimble to compete with new energy competitors and the possibility of utility deregulation not seen in its century of operations. I was able to introduce innovative strategic planning techniques such as diverse thought leader forums. I developed skills in bringing together executive teams spanning organizational boundaries to examine industry trends, emerging threats, and competitive intelligence.

In this public utility environment, I discovered the thrill of witnessing leaders thinking deeply and collectively about the future of their organization. I saw firsthand how interdisciplinary brainpower became the most *vital* part of the strategic planning process. I learned how well-curated activities and important conversations could help the executive team put aside individual agendas and unify their focus on the future.

This valuable experience provided great insight as I moved into an executive position as vice provost at Arizona State University. The idea of including external strategic planning guest participants for the institutional advancement division was unheard of. I knew that candid constituent input was critically important to help the university's institutional advancement department be attuned to community needs and hopes, and to use this valuable input to shape strategic goals. Within a few years, my assigned campus featuring four colleges doubled in student enrollment—and tripled in donor contributions.

A few years later, I served as a nonprofit healthcare president and CEO. The organization was in its second decade with many opportunities ahead, but it lacked a strategic plan. I worked closely with my board of directors to change that.

My first strategic plan served as a beacon of light for the agency's survival during the chaotic financial downturn of 2008 through 2011. In 2013, my second strategic plan led to the successful development of a 55,000-square-foot community health and research center supported by private donor investments and a multimillion-dollar municipal bond. Both strategic plans began the same way—with an engaging board and executive planning workshop, followed by a well-written plan that was rigorously tracked, discussed with board and staff, and communicated externally.

My experience led to a success framework for many other planning projects resulting in strategic impact, including one for a city's ten-year general plan approved by city voters. Leading up to the vote, hundreds of community engagement workshops and website interactions were hosted for input gathering. This was followed by writing and community vetting processes. The final written plan was managed and tracked by city planning department staff.

Through the years, I've learned that strategic planning is an intense human experience. And that's why I wrote this book.

YOU ARE A LIFE CHANGER

So . . . *you're* the one responsible for leading your organization's strategic plan.

Whether you're an executive, a consultant, an emerging leader, or a board member, if you are in charge of your organization's strategic plan, I wrote this book for *you*—the strategic planning genius. The organization you're planning for may be a client—or it may be the company where you work. No matter what type of organization it is, you're going to be a *life changer* for it.

All types of organizations need strategic plans, but it's crucial to be aware that there is a minefield of *unsuccessful* approaches to this planning. I'm a strategic planning executive and consultant who has worked for nearly three decades with corporate, nonprofit, governing, and trade-association clients. Along the way, I've heard my share of nightmare strategic planning stories. In today's world, no organization can afford scenarios that give strategic planning a bad rap.

All-Too-Common Strategic Planning Nightmares

- The poorly facilitated workshop where leaders are brought together with unskilled facilitation and end up wasting time analyzing and arguing about operational tactics while the company forges ahead in the wrong direction.

- The hyped-up planning event filled with rhetoric but no follow-up. The workshop seemed too good to be true . . . and in fact, it was!

---

continued

- The workshop where the CEO or members of the executive team arrive late or not at all. Or, they arrive but are constantly stepping out of the room to take phone calls.

- The grandiose strategic plan put together by a corporate planning department where goals may be gilded and set in stone but are never effectively communicated, tracked, or tied to departments, actions, dates, or people.

- The mystery plan, where a tight circle of executives meet in secret. Their covert mission ends with the plan being sprung on the employees. The planning team is justifiably stunned by management's complete lack of transparency, and views the whole operation with a healthy dose of suspicion.

- The company that pursues a strategic plan as a formality, and assigns someone to "go write the plan." The resulting plan is an isolated, inauthentic bunch of boring documents—read by no one—and quickly becomes a shelf ornament, just as it was designed to be.

- Finally, there's the prolonged, stalled, or completely shut down strategic planning process that results in no plan but costs lots of time and money. This occurs when expensive strategic planning consultants drag out the process for months and charge outrageous fees as they conduct unproductive meetings.

If any of this sounds familiar, read on. My intent in writing this book is twofold.

First, I will offer you an exciting, three-part strategic planning framework for *your* organization in a way that will transform what is normally a dreaded obligation into a *vital and unifying leadership team experience* crucial to your company's future.

Second, I will help you create a useful strategic plan that gets implemented and moves your company forward to great success.

I'll do both of these things while debunking the myth that strategic planning requires expensive consultants and budget-breaking, complicated planning processes (seemingly led by the Wizard of Oz behind a curtain).

A THREE-PART FRAMEWORK FOR GOING FORWARD

Strategic Impact provides a three-part framework to guide your planning focus.

1. Customizable Structure for Your Strategic Planning Workshop

A customizable structure for a vibrant workshop will help you develop a meaningful strategic planning leadership experience that is expertly custom crafted for your organization. This workshop structure includes insights and new opportunities for a hybrid state of strategic planning, where meetings may be held virtually as well as in person, driven by our world's distributed, work-from-home environment that became essential during the COVID-19 global pandemic.

2. Customizable Written Strategic Plan Framework

An easy-to-use-and-adapt written plan framework will aid in producing your organization's unique and customized written strategic plan, both in hard copy and digital formats.

3. Practical and Customizable System for Tracking and Communicating Results

Strategic Impact covers what most strategic planning primers completely miss—support for your organization's implementation program. Implementation includes the means to track, communicate, and celebrate your organization's strategic planning results, and do it in a way that is *meaningful and practical* for your organization.

You are the strategic planning expert. Unlike complicated strategic planning textbooks, this book *supports you*—the person who is responsible and in the life-changing business—to guide your organization through each of the three critical parts of a *vital* strategic planning process: your workshop, your written plan, and your tracking and communication system.

And by doing this process well, you will help your organization simplify the process, save time, and cut unnecessary planning costs.

I believe that the genius of *Strategic Impact* is the part played by *you*, the curator or facilitator. Even more essential, your genius will help unlock the *collective genius* of your organization, or the client organizations you serve. I suggest reading chapter 1 and then jumping to the chapters that are most useful for you and your organization.

CHAPTER 1

IT'S TIME TO
SIMPLIFY THE PROCESS

MOST EXECUTIVES SAY THEY DREAD STRATEGIC planning. Yet truly effective strategic planning should be life *changing* for the participants and life *giving* for the organization. Strategic planning studies during the past two decades have shown that more than half of global company executives are very dissatisfied with their organization's strategic planning programs. Less than 20 percent of employees—one in five—have a good understanding of their company's strategy and direction.[1] Leaders commonly describe strategic planning with words such as:

- "being lost in a haze, with no way out"

- "boring"

- "too complicated"

- "creating a shelf ornament"

- "lofty, but no implementation"

- "a mysterious process"

- "paying more than $300,000 to a management consulting firm that didn't know what it was doing."

So what do we need to do?

Most executives are excellent at running their organizations, but may not be quite sure how to develop an exciting leadership experience that will lead to a successful strategic plan and—most crucial—implementation. It's important to consider your strategic plan as your company's grand employee engagement tool leading to strategic impact for the organization, as well as for each individual employee.

Strategic impact is the ability to significantly and positively influence the future by achieving goals.

STRATEGIC IMPACT IS THE ABILITY OF:

AN ORGANIZATION,
BUSINESS UNIT,
DEPARTMENT,
AND EVERY EMPLOYEE TO
SIGNIFICANTLY AND POSITIVELY INFLUENCE
THE FUTURE BY ACHIEVING GOALS.

According to a recent employee mindset study, only one out of every ten employees says their overall work experience significantly exceeds their expectations. Only 38 percent would consider their employee experience as "awesome" or "great."[2] With a clear and compelling strategic plan combined with management training to help those in supervisory roles be equipped to share, regularly discuss, and track the plan throughout the organization, leaders can help employees understand how their work connects to their organization's purpose and creates strategic impact.

Employees want to know how their work connects to their organization's future success. They not only want to be passionate about their work; they also want an *employee experience* that will move them toward a business partnership culture where each employee views their work as an entrepreneur does—as their own business. This kind of mindset creates loyalty and stronger partnerships with managers and team members.

Strategic planning *should be* a legacy-making, destiny-defining experience for company leaders and employees. It's time to simplify the strategic planning process and, equally important, create richer, more meaningful strategic planning experiences.

WHAT IS STRATEGIC PLANNING?

The strategic planning process is a structured method of identifying and establishing a long-term vision for an organization to achieve its desired strategic goals. The process includes defining the organization's vision and mission; developing strategic goals; crafting action steps to realize those goals; and developing plans for action, monitoring, and accountability.[3] In addition, I believe vital strategic planning includes effectively communicating with—and celebrating results with—employees as well as with external audiences.

It's been said that the twin hallmarks of strategic planning are the great size of the decisions, and their long-term significance over many years. Strategic planning should not be confused with business planning, annual operational planning, forecasting, or budgeting.[4]

What is strategy? Strategy is the process of making choices about the business you're in, what you're delivering, as well as what your organization has no intention of providing. Strategy is a framework for making decisions about how goals will be accomplished and deliver value and competitive edge, for which customers or service clients are willing to pay.

Strategic planning includes difficult strategy choices—choices about the "how" that drive market differentiation and competitive advantage, as well as choices that enable an organization to operate with revenue and profits. Difficult strategy choices could include capital investments, marketing methods defining how you will reach customers, and sales approaches such as how products, programs, and services will be delivered.

Clearly, strategic plans differ from operational plans, marketing plans, and business plans.

The most important difference between a written strategic plan and an operational plan is its time frame. Strategic plans feature longer-term goals than operational plans and are usually focused on a three-year time horizon. Some market sectors, such as information technology, may require shorter strategic plan time frames.

The essential elements of a strategic plan include a thorough review of the external environment impacting your organization, a description of the current state of your organization, a description of the desired future within a three-year period or time horizon appropriate for your industry and organization, and finally, specific and measurable goals to help your organization achieve that desired future.

An operational plan features annual goals. An operating plan, also known as "annual operating plan," helps you look at the next year ahead and moves your organization toward achieving the strategic three-year goals. The strategy of "how" goals are achieved, including decisions about allocating resources to support the goals, such as expertise, funding, technology, and facilities, must be discussed with both strategic or longer-term and annual operating time frames in mind.

A marketing plan is a document that outlines promotional and advertising strategy that an organization will implement to generate customer leads and reach its target markets. A marketing plan spells out the promotional, communication, and public relations activities to be undertaken over a particular time period, noting how the company will measure the effect of the marketing initiatives. An organization's go-to-market strategy uses internal sales representatives and outside distributors to deliver their unique value proposition to customers or clients, and achieve competitive advantage.

For anyone starting a business, developing a business plan is an important first step. A business plan is used to initially obtain funding and provide direction for business operations.

While a strategic plan is focused on a longer horizon of three to five years and shares a few common features with a business plan, the business plan is a defining document usually focused on the next twelve months—especially during the initial business start-up. A traditional business plan defines the operational purpose of the business. It summarizes financial objectives, including a detailed plan providing information about how the business will make money, and outlines projected revenues and expenses for the next few years.

What It Is and What It Isn't

To build upon these working definitions, I'm including some of my favorite strategic planning authors and their quotes. These prolific planners describe the essence of strategic planning . . . what it *is*, and what it is *not*.

"Strategic Planning is a disciplined effort to produce decisions and actions that shape and guide what an organization is, what it does, and why it does it."

—**John M. Bryson,** *Strategic Planning for Public and Nonprofit Organizations*

---

continued

"Strategic planning encourages new perspectives and new combinations of ideas that surpass departmental silos. However, strategic planning is imperfect . . . it cannot replace common sense and keen market awareness."

—**Henry Mintzberg,** *The Rise and Fall of Strategic Planning*

"Successful strategic planning includes addressing the ability of the organization to respond to its external environment. It forces thinking about the future. It focuses on the organization's challenges and identifies opportunities to address those challenges."

—**Henry Cothran and Rodney Clouser,** *Strategic Planning for Communities, Non-profit Organizations and Public Agencies*

"Strategic decisions and strategic goals alter the very destiny of the organization, pushing senior executives to contribute at the strategic level, where their input is most needed."

—**Harvey Bergholz,** *4 Ways to Keep Strategic Planning Focused*

"Strategy is about helping leaders solve a unique problem in their own organizational context, while also preparing them for a different future."

—**Ruth Tearle,** *Strategy for CEOs*

"Strategic planning can bring significant advantages such as higher profits and return on assets."

—**Stephen P. Robbins, Mary Coulter, and David A. DeCenzo,** *Fundamentals of Management*

WHAT MAKES A COMPANY SEEK A STRATEGIC PLAN?

When do companies typically embark on a strategic planning program? It is generally when the organization completes a prior strategic plan—or whenever leaders need to reinvent the future of their organization. In fact, strategic planning is all about reinventing the future.

Reinventing the future includes clarifying a management team's strategic priorities; establishing a clear path for growth, potential diversification, and sustainability; and setting clear goals for management.[5] This also may include responding to changing market conditions such as new or emerging competition, an industry crisis, a game-changing scientific discovery, or a global event such as COVID-19. The need for strategic planning is also critical after mergers and acquisitions, when fresh vision and a new company identity must be forged. Strategic planning frequently occurs upon the arrival of a new CEO with a new vision for an organization. In fact, within the first hundred days, most CEOs announce a new strategy after conducting a strategic planning process.

Almost every new CEO struggles to manage the time drain of attending to shareholders, analysts, board members, industry groups, politicians, and other constituencies.[6] While CEOs hired from the outside have a learning curve, those promoted from within face their own set of challenges. They must separate themselves from CEOs of the past, as well as divorce themselves from their own prior roles within the company. New leaders can build professional momentum and credibility by creating an engaging strategic planning process as an opportunity to bond with board members and staff and gain employee support for their new vision and direction.

Occasionally, a new CEO will be hired into an organization with no existing strategic plan. This can become a fortuitous opportunity for the new CEO.

This often happens when a start-up company is launched by a passionate founder with no strategic plan, where the company gains its first round of success, begins to scale up, and hires an experienced executive to manage the growth. It can also occur when a long-standing family business or nonprofit organization hires a new leader after a predecessor served for decades without a strategic plan. (Think about a century-old trade association, for example, that hires a new CEO after the organization had operated for decades with a list of annual goals, but no official strategic plan.)

New leaders know that developing a strategic plan will require support from the board of directors. However, a skeptical board member may question the need for the plan. Instead of avoiding the naysayer, if the new CEO is wise, he or she will invite the skeptic to serve on the strategic planning steering committee as it reviews the workshop agenda and provides input. That is, unless the questioning board member is a toxic derailer—someone who tries to sabotage the entire strategic planning process. In those circumstances, a strong and supportive steering committee will need to address the negativity directly with the sabotaging board member.

The workshop planning process may take a few months due to difficulty of scheduling the steering committee. But after rounds of discussions and edits, the agenda is eventually approved, and even the skeptical board member is onboard with his peers. The CEO moves forward with a vital strategic planning program, confident that the board provided full support.

The lesson learned in this scenario is that critical thinkers can play an important role in helping you, the new leader, shape your strategic planning program and cultivate enthusiasm among the full board of directors. Build a majority of supporters to take the naysayers under their wings. When you vet your workshop agenda through a steering committee, it will help you build buy-in for your strategic planning program. It also can help you win over critics.

WHAT DOES A PLANNING FRAMEWORK NEED?

Vital strategic planning should be kept as simple as possible. I present three essential, vital requirements in the following framework.

VITAL STRATEGIC PLANNING =

THE STRATEGIC PLANNING WORKSHOP
(THE SHARED LEADERSHIP EXPERIENCE)

+

THE WRITTEN STRATEGIC PLAN
(THE SHARED STORY OF STRATEGIC INTENT)

+

THE SYSTEM FOR TRACKING
AND COMMUNICATING RESULTS
(THE SHARED GOAL OUTCOMES—THIS IS STRATEGIC IMPACT)

This three-step framework is what I call the Vital Strategic Plan. My Vital Strategic Plan incorporates best practices and key principles that shape the core body of knowledge for global strategic planning professionals. According to the Association for Strategic Planning, these include strategic leadership, strategic thinking, strategic planning, strategic actions, and desired results.[7]

While stepping around the "old castles" of complex and mysterious strategic planning, I'm erecting a "new tent" in combining three strategic planning building blocks, according to Rosabeth Moss Kanter—starting with the workshop, continuing with a vibrant written plan, and culminating with effective tracking and communication.[8] This novel, three-part approach will create opportunities to include new leaders and diverse, typically unheard voices that go beyond the CEO suite. With the Vital Strategic Plan model, your organization's strategic plan will become critically relevant to its future success.

Your Workshop (the Shared Experience)

A vital strategic planning workshop will prepare participants to become the best strategic, cross-functional leaders they can be. All great strategic plans begin with a compelling workshop—a shared human leadership experience. By using an adaptable workshop framework, you can customize a strategy-focused workshop to meet the needs of almost any organization. This time-saver will reduce the need for expensive consultants and allow you to put more focus on the quality of strategic planning interaction, content, and outcomes—rather than structure.

The idea that a vibrant strategic planning workshop is the most important first strategy step for any meaningful strategic plan—as a treasured, bonding, and indispensable leadership experience—flies in the face of conventional strategic planning.

The workshop itself can and should be life changing. By that I mean that the workshop you conduct can and should lead to lifelong friendships, teamwork, and an unwavering commitment to work together toward a shared vision for your organization's future success. In this book, I place enormous focus on carefully curating and delivering a powerful planning workshop for your executive team. This leadership experience can then be extended to all levels of your organization, creating a unifying experience throughout your firm.

At Arizona State University, I was part of the executive team charged with leading a strategic plan for each of the university's colleges spanning four campuses. First, we invited each college dean to form a college "big idea" planning committee. Each college dean was charged with developing visionary program ideas based on each college's distinct competencies. Once the big ideas were shaped, fundraising case for support documents would be developed.

Each college dean selected a diverse representation of faculty, staff, and students. This created an inclusive process that extended beyond college management. Groups examined colleges across the United States and assessed their own college's strengths, weaknesses, and opportunities. This allowed each college to define degree programs of unique distinction not duplicated in other universities. This participative approach created internal pride in each college's most competitive programs. It also created focus on opportunities for program improvement.

Each team then was charged with developing big ideas for their college's programs of distinction. University participants knew that in order for a big program idea to be implemented, it had to meet ideation criteria. This created a vulnerable idea-generating experience in a distributed workshop environment across the university.

Many of our visionary cases for support papers became the foundation for more than $2 billion raised during the university's multiyear campaign. The participative workshop strategy process engaged the entire university and led to big projects, new donors, community engagement, and strategic impact.

What defines a unifying workshop experience where participants feel comfortable being their authentic selves and exposing creativity in a vulnerable way? Strategy guru Henry Mintzberg discusses the thrill of bringing together great thinkers or gathering humans with sharp minds to examine trends and shape strategy to detect what he calls "subtle discontinuities," or an underlying movement that may undermine a business in the future.[9]

Mintzberg differentiated strategic planning from strategic thinking. Strategic planning focuses on structured analysis and learning from the analysis. Strategic thinking, in contrast, is about *synthesis*. Synthesis, he emphasized, involves intuition and creativity, and this cannot be overcalculated and formalized, nor can it be forced into the parameters of a strategic planning retreat. He said, "Strategy making is an immensely complex process, which involves the most sophisticated, subtle, and, at times, subconscious elements of human thinking."[10]

Yet leaders do need to come together to plan for their organization's future, often under great time constraints and monumental scheduling challenges. Shared strategic thinking requires the ability to learn from data and synthesize trends to creatively envision the future. It requires a level of candid, unvarnished assessment rather than an excessively cheerful or optimistic view. This examination also requires a high level of trust among the strategic planning team.

In the case of the ASU example, each college dean brought great thinkers together. Some were faculty, staff, and students who had never been invited to participate in a big idea workshop process. From the start, ground rules included the need to focus on the college's visionary future—and not overanalyze the merit of each individual concept during the ideation stage. This created a safe space and allowed permission to maximize strengths, while also addressing underlying issues and difficult topics such as declining enrollments and challenges with faculty recruitment in a few lackluster programs. Deans invited critical thinking—analysis and input that might be otherwise misinterpreted as negative thinking. This built a new level of excitement, trust, and camaraderie throughout the university.

More recently, post COVID-19, we saw a dramatic shift toward distributed workplaces—a perfect example of Mintzberg's discontinuities, but these were unpredictable altogether. With no time to prepare, companies immediately pivoted to social distancing. Employees worked at home or in isolated job settings. The pandemic wreaked havoc with the commercial real estate industry across the globe, where significant numbers of leased commercial workspaces were suddenly empty, leaving a long-term mark.

Urbanists are wise to explore the question of whether this will change the trajectory of commercial and urban development, resulting in more people working from their homes in hubs outside of large cities. Only time will tell.

I strongly believe that your strategic planning workshop is paramount to your entire strategic planning program. As strategic plan curators, it's a great privilege and responsibility to create the thrill and anticipation that Mintzberg notes as you bring together great thinkers. The quality of your workshop and the richness of its discovery, dialogue, and debate will drive the vibrancy of your written plan and the way the plan is implemented, tracked, communicated, and celebrated. This is why a vital workshop must be customized. It must meet the specific needs of your organization.

In addition to bringing together great minds, a vital strategic planning workshop helps participants look outwardly first. It forces them to examine the external trends and pressures impacting your business before the group turns inward. When your leadership team understands your industry's external world, then—and only then—can they be prepared to examine internal issues and chart your organization's strategic path forward.

A trade association's board of directors spotted a downward spiral in memberships and event participation. In examining other trade associations, the board discovered that this was an international trend due to the availability of online webinars and training. This bit of external analysis revealed an opportunity to introduce online workshops, podcasts, and other web-based continuing education programs to complement its traditional in-person membership meetings. This strategy doubled attendance while boosting program revenues.

Your Written Strategic Plan (the Shared Story of Strategic Intent)

Your written strategic plan is your organization's story of *now* and the *near future*. Your strategic plan should be an organization's compelling, living and breathing story that can be embodied by its people. This is not a shelf ornament—something that looks good but sits idle as a showpiece in a cabinet. The purpose of a written plan is to start the ball rolling, to get things moving not only toward a brilliant future for your organization, but to communicate strategic intent (stated goals) that will provide your organization with the opportunity to produce strategic impact (results).

YOUR ORGANIZATION'S WRITTEN STRATEGIC PLAN PROVIDES A SHARED STORY ABOUT YOUR ORGANIZATION'S GOALS.

GOALS CREATE STRATEGIC INTENT.

––––––

YOUR ORGANIZATION'S SYSTEM FOR TRACKING AND COMMUNICATING GOAL PROGRESS PROVES YOUR ORGANIZATION'S STRATEGIC IMPACT.

TRACKED GOALS AND COMMUNICATED RESULTS CREATE STRATEGIC IMPACT.

––––––

A colleague once said, "Where attention goes, energy flows," and she is right. Strategic intention needs *attention* to result in strategic impact. Written plans can sharpen employee focus as well as re-energize an organization's constituents.

For example, a renowned private school operating in the United

States since the early 1800s had been in a state of quiet transition. While important planning work was underway, the locals were aware. However, the academy's broader communication to alumni and donors across the globe had been dormant for nearly two years. This important external audience was totally in the dark about the institution's progress, and they began questioning the school's leadership, direction, and financial health.

Finally, when the strategic plan was completed, the academy distributed a magazine-style version of the strategic plan titled *Strategic Vision* to every donor, alumni family, and community leader. The plan featured recent successes, along with a listing of the vision, mission, values, and key goal areas, including student experience, a focus on educational programs, attracting quality facility and staff, master campus planning, and financial strength. The head of the school issued a promise to further engage with readers. The school's written plan rebuilt confidence and jump-started constituent engagement after a long period of lull.

> **YOUR WRITTEN PLAN SUMMARIZES** YOUR ORGANIZATION'S PRIORITIZED STRATEGIC GOALS— YOUR ORGANIZATION'S STRATEGIC INTENT OF WHAT NEEDS TO BE ACCOMPLISHED.

Strategic intent is further operationalized on a daily, weekly, monthly, and yearly basis through your organization's annual goals— breaking it down to what gets done in the next twelve months—in other words, strategic intent for the next year.

Both longer-term strategic and twelve-month annual goals provide direction and focus for your organization's strategic *intent*. Then, *strategic impact* is revealed when both annual and strategic goal results are tracked, and when the results—or proof of achievements—are then communicated and celebrated.

A vital written strategic plan guides decisions that determine *what* your organization is and does, *who* it serves, and *where* it's going in the next few years. It engages your entire work force in a meaningful way and communicates with visual infographics and animated diagrams.

A vital written plan includes strategic, multiyear goals, such as goals with a three-year time frame. Strategic goals are further broken into well-articulated annual, twelve-month operating goals. Most organizations provide monthly, quarterly, and final annual progress reports summarizing annual goal process.

Here's how the written plan evolves, from start to finish. During your strategic planning workshop, someone should be appointed to take notes, including a recap of all flip charts where ideas are captured.

The workshop is the place to identify and discuss external trends and develop prioritized strategic goals. At the conclusion of the workshop, everyone should have gained a clear sense of your organization's strategic goal priorities. Staff can help you capture the discussion and flip-chart notes. These will be summarized offline as raw notes, and these notes will further be edited into the final written document, using my strategic plan framework (to be discussed later). Whether written by you or by a hired writer, the raw workshop notes will become the foundation for the more eloquent written strategic plan document.

I often hire a writer to accompany me when I facilitate strategic planning workshops. During the workshop, my writer will help me accurately summarize all the plenary discussions in real time. Later, I sift through the workshop notes and finalize the written plan.

Again, the written plan will *not* be written at the workshop. Following the workshop, you or the assigned writer will use the workshop summary notes to draft your organization's written strategic plan. Your writer will compile meeting notes, including workshop presentations and any relevant diagrams and charts, as well as flip-chart notes from plenary and breakout sessions. This workshop recap will become an important raw summary for your organization's records. Parts of your workshop summary not used in the strategic plan may become excellent resources to include in the written plan's appendix.

The outline provided in this book provides a customizable written plan framework to assist you and your organization in producing an engaging, comprehensive strategic plan story for your organization. Edit the outline as needed. Provide customized sections based on your organization's need to share strategy. With a flexible blueprint guiding your written plan, you can spend more time focused on developing the compelling content and less time on creating the written format. You or your writer can take the workshop meeting notes and distill the most important points, using the written strategic plan outline provided in chapter 5 to guide the flow of the written information. A vital written strategic plan is:

- Held in high stature as the guiding vision for your company's future.

- Your company's strategy road map for a multiyear time period—usually three years, due to our world's rapidly changing environment.

- Vital to both short-term *and* long-term success of your organization, because it envisions a desired future.

- Viewed as a flexible guide to future success—and is updated as needed.

- Compelling, customized, and exceptionally written.

- A catalyst for enhancing employee purpose and loyalty, because it brings all employees together with an understanding of where your organization is headed.

- Promoted internally throughout the company to all employees.

- Promoted externally at a high level, with focus on engaging customers and community constituents, to create market buzz and positive public relations.

- Is produced in both hard copy and digital versions, and becomes a platform for blogs, podcasts, social media posts, and featured articles.

Your System for Tracking and Communicating Results (Shared Strategic Impact)

Prior to the production of your written strategic plan, you will want to help your organization select an effective system to track and communicate strategic ongoing goal progress. It's important to keep in mind that your organization's tracking report is an essential tool for documenting strategic impact.

Chapter 6 presents tracking options, from simple spreadsheets for smaller organizations to collaborative, digital tracking systems available through subscriptions. Thanks to these cloud-based online tracking tools, it's easier than ever to track and measure your organization's strategic plan goal progress. Small organizations with limited budgets may prefer to use a simple spreadsheet. When you effectively track goal progress, communicate, and celebrate when goals are achieved, you are demonstrating leadership's commitment to implementing the written strategic plan.

After your written strategic plan is developed, a communication plan should be created to provide communication support for your organization's strategic plan. As a separate support document to the written strategic plan, a strategic *communication* plan aligns an organization's communication and marketing strategies and tactics to support the organization's goals. Be sure to include communication staff from the get-go as part of your strategic planning team. Effective communication supports employee understanding and engagement. Your communication staff will be a key partner for developing a communication plan to spotlight ongoing goal progress and to support candid company-wide conversations about enterprise-level goals.

This could include employee forums discussing the strategic plan, as well as a series of articles discussing the organization's strategic goals. Specific departments could be featured to showcase how work groups are achieving goal progress—and to explore real challenges.

Tracking tools can be designed to report individual, department, and enterprise-level progress—and this is a significant form of communication showing goal progress. Goal-tracking combined with planned, deliberate internal communication is a useful recipe for helping employees understand how their daily work contributes to the strategic plan and company success.

What Gets Tracked? Goals Developed to Support These Four Strategic Pillars

1. Your organization's Programs, Products, and Services.

2. Financial—resources including operating revenue, donor contributions, and income from producing products and services.

3. Operational Effectiveness—any department leading to effective processing of internal business *within* an organization, such as Human Resources (HR) and Information Technology (IT).

4. External Outreach—Communication, Marketing, and Branding, all outward-facing activities promoting the company and its brand.

As you curate your company's strategic planning program, I highly recommend the following Leadership Map as an effective visual diagram to enhance your workshop and written plan. I like this map because it's simple and easy to grasp. Leadership maps are excellent tools for showing how your organization's vision, mission, strategic pillars, strategic goals, and annual operating goals are connected.

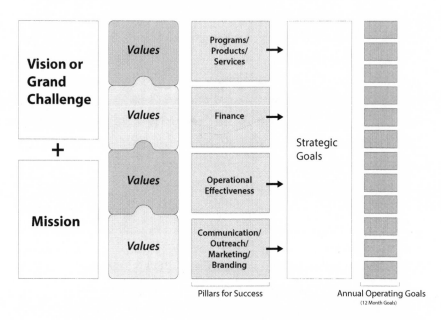

Leadership Map template. See more information about using leadership maps in the appendix.

Leadership Map © Carol A. Poore

HOW DO ORGANIZATIONS OF DIFFERENT SIZES APPROACH STRATEGIC PLANNING?

Organizations approach the process of strategic planning in different ways.

Some organizations prefer to take a hybrid approach, where key internal leaders tap outside consultants for strategic planning niche expertise. This could include engaging stakeholders in the process to understand their needs and concerns, as well as extensive trend analysis that goes beyond the capacity of employees and volunteer board members whose jobs are not focused on strategic planning. While leaders within an organization can provide the advantage of knowing their organization's business dynamics and culture, external consultants may bring helpful techniques and analytical tools for a more thorough planning process.

For example, a small family-owned restaurant business or chamber of commerce may budget funds to hire a consultant to manage some or all of the strategic planning framework (workshop, written plan, goal-tracking, and communication). Beginning with the workshop, the consultant would manage the strategic planning program and logistics, while working closely with key leaders throughout the process.

In reality, however, very few small businesses and nonprofits plan the needed budget to hire a strategic planning consultant. Even when there's technically no budget, I encourage nonprofit organizations of all sizes to creatively seek capacity-building grants or donor underwriting to sponsor a strategic planning firm or consultant. A well-matched consultant can bring expertise for efficiently shaping and facilitating the workshop, drafting the written plan, and shaping the plan for tracking and ongoing communication.

In the United States, there are nearly 200,000 midmarket businesses with revenues between $10 million and $1 billion, according to the National Center for the Middle Market. These businesses include internet travel industry leader Trip Advisor, health-focused grocery store chain Sprouts Farmers Market, fast food chains such as Chick-fil-A, and local hospitals and car dealerships.

Midmarket firms represent one-third of the private sector US gross domestic product. Leaders of midsized organizations often assign the strategic planning role to an internal executive accountable for vetting, hiring, and overseeing the work of a strategic planning consultant or consultant firm. As a direct report to the CEO or a senior executive, and as an ambassador for strategic planning throughout the organization, the internal strategic planning leader serves as the point person for the planning consultant, and work is shared between the consultant and internal staff.

Rather than take a top-down approach where the strategic plan workshop is shaped by a few executive managers and dictated to the rest of the company, many multilocation companies and franchises, including hotel and restaurant chains, combine a corporate, top-down approach with a location-specific, bottoms-up workshop and input approach, creating localization and adaptability of the strategic plan. This creates a flexible, inclusive model of seeking employee participation. While the corporate planning process may begin at corporate headquarters, leaders and employees in multiple cities can participate, whether in small groups or in today's world, on digital platforms such as Zoom or Webex.

Large companies earning revenues of more than $1 billion often feature planning departments typically organized within corporate planning, finance, or marketing divisions. Large companies, such as food delivery service Door Dash and shared workspace and real estate firm WeWork, grew from start-up to large status in less than five years.

Large-company planning requires a formal process. A detailed calendar will show key deadlines for each department to submit plans for contribution to the overarching strategic plan. The planning process is usually done at the same time each year, often several months before the next fiscal year. Large companies usually develop a formalized process or playbook shared with all department leaders. This calendar and set of procedures may be repeated from year to year, but the planning cycle will be updated by staff as needed to fit the organization's needs.

Large companies can generate a large quantity of data to assist with the planning process. Planning staff may supplement internal forecasting by hiring outside research firms, or purchasing subscription-based trend reports and market analysis.

Planning is a major function of municipalities—also considered as large organizations. Most city government structures have a planning department dedicated to carrying out long- and short-term development plans.

Phoenix Planning Process

Vital strategic planning can and does take place in a variety of settings, including municipalities. For the city of Phoenix, for example, I was involved in a community leadership committee tapped to provide guidance for a citywide planning process impacting transportation and land use, arts and culture, housing, neighborhoods, public facilities, natural resources, and energy. In Arizona, every city is required by state law to develop a ten-year general plan or update an existing plan, and the plan must be approved by a majority of voters by public vote. A general plan provides the vision and policies that determine how a city will grow and develop.

---

continued

I helped lead a volunteer community leadership committee that worked closely with city staff and hosted "PlanPHX" public meetings and visioning workshops. The face-to-face programs spanned three years, starting with a massive series of public workshops focused on community visioning. The city advertised public meetings that were held in community facilities in every city district. Some of the sessions included bilingual facilitators to ensure broad-based input and inclusion.

For the first round of meetings, we asked participants one question: What's your big idea for Phoenix? All ideas were welcome—big and small. Thousands of residents contributed ideas through the city's website and by traditional mail delivery. Then, something magic—something *vital*—happened when all of the ideas were categorized, and five major themes emerged. The themes were: connect people and places, build the sustainable city, strengthen our local economy, celebrate our diverse communities and neighborhoods, and create an even more vibrant downtown.

Each major theme featured guiding principles, similar to a goal-setting process. With input from residents, the guiding principles provided specific direction to guide the city's future decade of development.

One of the city's five core values focused on connective transportation: "Connect People and Places." This theme put emphasis on transit-oriented development initiatives and access to a well-functioning light rail system, bike paths along the light rail, and walking paths on the city's water canals and in parks. Soon after the plan was approved, the city secured a multimillion-dollar grant from the federal government to add pedestrian infrastructure and lighting to several stretches of the Grand Canal in central Phoenix.

The theme "Celebrate Our Diverse Communities and Neighborhoods" focuses on enhancing existing established neighborhoods while combating urban sprawl. In response to the plan's goal of developing more affordable housing and activating underused property within the city's light rail corridor, the city secured a $30 million grant from the US Department of Housing and Urban Development to transform a local neighborhood community, Edison-Eastlake, into a vibrant mixed-income neighborhood. Within five years, more than twenty-five residential and mixed-use projects were approved, resulting in thousands of additional housing units in downtown.

A one-year writing and sharing process was put into place, after which Phoenix residents approved the updated general plan with more than 76 percent of voter support. The final written plan is posted on the city's website. Today, the city's planning staff meets regularly with residents in each city council district, discussing new initiatives and opportunities as well as tracking progress regarding the city's five core values or themes.

WHAT DOES AN EXCEPTIONAL STRATEGIC PLANNING CONSULTANT DO, AND WHY MIGHT YOU NEED ONE?

If you are charged with your organization's strategic plan, you may be the internal strategic planning leader or internal consultant responsible for the comprehensive program discussed in this chapter. Or, you may prefer to hire an exceptional strategic planning consultant who can work with you and the executive management and planning team to support decision making for all aspects of the Vital Strategic Plan framework.

An effective consultant is an investment into the future of your business, saving your organization time and money in the long term by producing an efficient and streamlined process.

The most compelling reasons to hire a strategic planning consultant include expertise and experience in working with organizations, speed and cost-effectiveness for efficiency (based on experience) versus hiring a full-time employee, objectivity and fresh thinking, and a focus on project management to keep your strategic planning program on track and adhering to your strategic planning timeline.

I've found, as have other strategic planning experts, that effective strategic planning integrates strategy development and skillful facilitation of deep-dive strategy conversations and decision making about strategic goals.

If you hire only a facilitator, important strategy discussions may be completely missed. If you hire only a strategist, difficult goal decision conversations may be missed—the kind that result in leaders taking ownership of their organization's strategic plan.[11]

Even if your organization hires a strategic planning consultant who is both strategist and facilitator, it's not uncommon for consultants to tap a separate workshop facilitator, such as a company's internal expert, to lead portions of the conversation. This can add variety to meetings and supplement the consultant's skills.

Here's an important point to always remember—the consultant does not own the strategic plan. Your organization's executive team and employees do!

A capable, competent strategic planning consultant will steward the process but will not attempt to "own" the process or keep the client organization's executive team at arm's length. Rather, an exceptional consultant will come alongside the executive team and help structure deep-dive strategy discussions, as well as prompt team decisions so that each leader takes ownership for their company's future.

Valuable consulting services may include:

- Meeting with an organization's chief executive or executive team to help structure a vibrant program using the three-part framework, and build executive team confidence in the strategic process and timeline.

- Engaging the organization in assessments and needed pre-workshop research.

- Planning the workshop and all pre-workshop analysis activities, working with executive staff and whoever within an organization is commissioning the strategic planning program.

- Either before, during, or after the strategic planning workshop, using analysis and research to lead deeper-dive discussions and advising the executive team about data-driven business strategy, serving as a catalyst for *their* conclusions and decisions.

- Facilitating and documenting all strategic planning meetings related to the strategic plan.

- Helping the planning team develop clear and measurable goals based on data.

- Drafting the written strategic plan.

- Helping the organization develop a communication plan to support the executive team's internal (employee) and external (constituents) communication efforts. This could include working with the organization's communication staff or point person.

- Helping the organization assess and select a strategic plan tracking and reporting system.

———

Thorough Does Not Mean Complicated

For critics who may assume that my three-part, easy-to-understand framework implies shortcuts or is too simplistic, rest assured that this is not the case. Great strategy is not something that can be rushed or forced into a cookie-cutter approach. And I believe effective strategic planning is not a one-time event, but rather includes an ongoing dialogue between leaders, employees, and the organization's relevant external constituents (such as customers, clients, patients, donors, alumni, neighborhood groups, and suppliers, to name a few).

The Vital Strategic Plan three-part framework defies the common belief that all significant strategic planning must be complicated and drawn out. The framework provides a rigorous and comprehensive approach to customizing a quality workshop, a written plan, and tracking and communication system. I shine a spotlight on each of the formula's three components to ensure nothing is overlooked or lost in the process.

The outcome? A clear understanding of your organization's strategic impact. This is where most strategic planning methods fall short. The third part of the framework—goal-tracking, communicating, and celebrating results—is equally as critical as the first two parts, because this third step proves your organization's strategic impact.

Customization for Large Organizations

The Vital Strategic Plan framework provides limitless ways you can customize each facet of your strategic planning program. If your organization is large and complex, you can choose to structure extensive pre-workshop analysis such as in-depth scenario-planning, financial modeling, and exercises to draw out a deeper level of dialogue and debate.

Substance and Simplicity for Smaller Businesses and Nonprofits

On the other hand, my framework offers both substance and simplicity for those 99 percent of smaller businesses and nonprofits not requiring a lengthy process. If your organization is small, you can choose to shape a fast-paced, super-efficient planning program to minimize costs and maximize everyone's time investment.

When it comes to strategy formation, you also can seek volunteer (donated) support to supplement staff resources.

When I served as CEO of a small-but-mighty healthcare nonprofit organization during the subprime mortgage crisis that triggered the US recession between 2008 and 2009, my agency faced a dire financial crisis as donors and funding sources were impacted after the collapse of a housing bubble, leading to mortgage delinquencies, foreclosures, and the devaluation of housing-related securities. Some of our donors lost homes and filed for bankruptcy.

At the onset of the crisis, the healthcare agency needed to develop emergency strategies and pivot quickly. We lacked the needed expertise on staff to complete scenario-planning for board direction. With the help of my board treasurer, I reached out to several nonprofit chief financial officers who were expert at scenario-planning. I invited them to become part of a two-week emergency ad-hoc committee. This working committee was charged with analyzing the healthcare nonprofit's financials and proposing three scenarios offering solutions for mitigating financial risk.

This donated brainpower otherwise would have cost my agency a six-figure stipend for the amount of work provided. Looking back, I clearly see how this working committee provided wisdom and momentum that helped to drive our turnaround at a pivotal moment, when so many other nonprofit organizations were going out of business.

CHAPTER 2

TEN STEPS TO SWIFTLY SECURE EXECUTIVE COMMITMENT

FOR YOU—THE STRATEGIC PLANNING LEADER—EVERY OPPORTUNITY to kick-start a vital strategic planning program should be a unique and exciting experience. Your first meeting with the chief executive or executive team will allow you to build their confidence in the planning process you are proposing—and in you as the strategic planning leader or consultant.

Before I ever meet with a top executive and anyone else he or she may invite, I fully research the company's website and online presence. Then, I prepare materials to help me guide a productive discussion, hitting all the key decision points I know will be needed to develop the workshop, the written plan, and the system for tracking, communication, and celebration. These decision points are noted in my ten preparation steps to follow.

Your first meeting with the executive team is immensely important. Your conversation should inspire the executive team to lead their strategic planning program with a great sense of urgency about the opportunity to create strategy and change for the future. A strategic planning program is a *transformation* program requiring executive urgency and company-wide solidarity. Business thought leader John Kotter noted that lack of urgency is the No. 1 reason why transformation efforts fail.[1] Kotter also talks about the importance of forming a powerful guiding coalition. Your organization's senior staff, along with the strategic planning steering committee, represent a committed coalition to lead the strategic planning change effort, working together as a unified and resilient team.

You can help your executive team lead with urgency. From the CEO to leaders of each division and department, unanimous support for their organization's strategic planning program will provide a positive and crucial driving force for ensuring their strategic planning program engages employees and leads to successful change. Their communication can emphasize the urgent need to examine such topics as competition, shrinking margins, decreasing market share, flat earnings, a lack of revenue growth, and a declining competitive position.

This chapter provides a road map for your first planning conversation with your organization's top executives. These guidelines will enable you to determine your own approach to confidently facilitate *their* important decisions. You'll arrive with a full arsenal of necessary discussion points and a method for covering the most important topics to get started.

PREPARATION IN TEN STEPS

Preparation is the key to your first successful executive discussion. With questions, talking points, and examples prepared in advance from my research, I can generally obtain most of the information I will need to draft a strategic planning approach and bring it back for the company's input and any possible revisions that might be needed. Most often I meet directly with the company's CEO, followed by a second meeting with the CEO and executive team. I recommend that you meet with the CEO and key staff from the get-go. This group might include senior leaders, strategic planners, and communication executives.

As the strategic planning consultant, your level of expertise and preparation has to be impressive. If it is, you'll be able to keep the planning discussion focused and on track.

In my experience as a strategic planning consultant and former CEO, the commitment to vital strategic planning always starts at the top, with the top executive and senior leadership team. Even for the most participative strategic planning processes, all planning efforts must begin with the full support and driving force of your organization's executive leadership. Executive leadership (including the board of directors) has to have skin in the game and be fully engaged in the three-part formula. This doesn't mean the *entire* strategic planning process must be top-down, nor does it exclude opportunities to engage all employees in strategic planning activities using a bottom-up approach.

You will be a much-needed coach and guide, and your firm leadership will help the executive committee make important decisions about the program that only they can make. You should be able to meet with your top executive or executive team and, within an hour, solicit important feedback allowing you to begin to plan your program.

If you or your consulting firm is hired by a company's planning department, or if you are a planning director in charge of your company's strategic planning process, or if you're invited by a well-meaning board member to lead the company's strategic planning session, here's my advice: do *not* embark on developing a strategic planning program until you've met with and vetted your program with your client's executive team and have incorporated their input. Executive management must *own* their strategic planning program.

Because that first meeting with my client or organization's executive team is so important, I always arrive with great expectation, knowing something *big* is on the horizon. I know that it's normal to experience a few butterflies of anticipation, because a lot of responsibility rests on my shoulders as the strategic planning expert. The success of my client's program rides on this very first conversation. This is why it is helpful to have a beginning framework from which to customize your strategic planning program. This will guide your discussion and expedite important decisions about the strategic planning program you'll eventually put in place for your client.

Consider these ten steps as you prepare to meet with your executive team.

STEP 1: PRESENT AND DISCUSS THE VITAL STRATEGIC PLAN FORMULA

After introductions and warm-up chat, I encourage you to start your meeting by discussing each part of the framework, with which you are now familiar:

VITAL STRATEGIC PLANNING =

THE STRATEGIC PLANNING WORKSHOP
(THE SHARED LEADERSHIP EXPERIENCE)

+

THE WRITTEN STRATEGIC PLAN
(THE SHARED STORY OF STRATEGIC INTENT)

+

**THE SYSTEM FOR TRACKING
AND COMMUNICATING RESULTS**
(THE SHARED GOAL OUTCOMES—THIS IS STRATEGIC IMPACT)

As you share this framework, stress the importance of executive leadership and, if applicable, board member participation throughout the entire course of strategic planning. Emphasize the importance of the workshop as a leadership team symposium or internal conference that fosters a shared learning experience. Then, help your executive team set goals for each of the three strategic planning formula components. Use the program goal worksheet at the end of this chapter as a handy discussion guide. The three-part formula is easy to understand, and your executive team will be impressed to learn that each part of the process will be driven by program expectations. During the workshop itself, it's important to include these goals in your agenda as well as on screen during your leader's opening welcome.

STEP 2: ASK RELEVANT, PROBING QUESTIONS

Once your client and leadership team have set goals and are warmed up for deeper discussion, take the consultant's approach and start asking questions. Select from the following sample questions to probe needs and gain insights for shaping the program. You can customize these questions to fit your situation.

- Does your organization already have an existing strategic plan? (If not, then you will be helping to charter your company's first plan from the ground up.)

- Ask the executive team to describe any pain points from prior strategic planning programs. Are there past issues or land mines, or problems under the surface to know about and avoid?

- What level of planning needs to be done—a refresh, or complete overhaul? (If the strategic plan was developed more than three years ago, it's time for a new plan.)

- What level of executive support exists for developing and implementing the strategic plan?

- Has the organization completed most of the goals from the prior strategic plan? (Skip this question if you already know the answer. Or, examine prior strategic goals to see if any are still relevant.)

- What competition and industry trends are reshaping your industry and your business?

- Has your organization recently found more success in providing new types of products or services?

- Is the organization floundering in any way?

- Who should be involved in the strategic planning sessions?

- Should we establish a steering committee to guide the strategic planning process?

STEP 3: GET A TEAM IN PLACE

The determination of *who* is involved in strategic planning is crucial to the success of the process as well as implementation of the plan. Seek input from the CEO and executive leadership team.

If the executive team is not going to be involved in providing detailed, day-to-day program feedback, ask your client to recommend a steering committee to serve as a helpful sounding board to periodically work alongside you throughout the strategic planning process. This executive-appointed committee can provide valuable guidance throughout the process and help you avoid organizational politics and potential land mines.

The ideal steering committee will be comprised of senior executives or their appointed leaders representing each division or department of the organization. If you can and it is appropriate, include several members of the board of directors.

I also recommend that you encourage your client to include emerging leaders who are influencers, as well as executives from human resources and communication departments. HR and communication departments are often left out of the process, but they are requisite support systems when it's time for ongoing implementation of the strategic plan. This increases the diversity of input and provides professional growth opportunities for the entire planning team.

STEP 4: DETERMINE THE BUDGET RIGHT OUT OF THE GATE

Discuss the budget and time commitment and staff support needed to support each piece of the Vital Strategic Plan framework. You'll need to know the estimated budget or spending limit for the strategic planning program's workshop, written plan, and tracking system. If this is initially unavailable, begin by discussing the workshop first. In the weeks that follow, you can lead the group to make budget decisions about publishing and communicating the written plan and developing the tracking system.

While your executive team may not know all the answers at this moment, they may share early recommendations that will help you plan an appropriate schedule. For certain types of industries such as healthcare, participants may need to coordinate shifts ahead of time in order to be in the same room.

STEP 5: DETERMINE THE WORKSHOP SCHEDULE AND LOCATION

You'll next want to decide on the workshop schedule and location depending on the type of organization and its·work culture and particular dynamics of your organization and agenda. For example, if your participants struggle to get away from their demanding work schedules, such as chief medical officers and nurse administrators employed by hospitals and medical clinics where it's difficult to be offsite for more than a work shift, a compressed one-day planning workshop may work best. Or, time permitting, a series of meetings may work best for your team. An offsite facility located nearby (not out of town) may be most practical, as well as cost-effective.

What amount of time can be reasonably allocated to complete a thorough and meaningful strategic planning workshop? How much time will it take to conduct your activities? Can one full day be allocated? Or will the planning workshop require two days, or possibly a series of strategic conversations spread out over several months culminating in a longer final session? Asking these questions early on will begin to help you customize an inclusive and realistic workshop schedule.

STEP 6: DISCUSS EXTERNAL SPEAKERS

When you meet with the executive team, present the idea of kicking off the strategic planning workshop with an opening panel. Share the benefits of this approach. Ask the question: Would a keynote speaker or expert panel enhance our discussion about external issues? Who might we invite to bring credible perspective about industry trends?

When you discuss the possibility of inviting external speakers to participate in your opening panel or presentation, some organizations may prefer to take an insular approach. But I highly recommend creating an opening external panel of experts to kick off your strategic planning workshop. I've found great success in inviting three to five panelists from the same field, trade association experts, well-known leaders, and industry celebrities in similar fields to talk about lessons learned that can be applied to your organization.

Significant benefits accrue when you open up a strategic planning workshop with invited experts. First, the expert panelists can share important insights that can set the tone and add moments of reflection for the remainder of your strategic planning workshop. For example, a panel of physicians representing private practice, a hospital association, and a state public health agency provided opening remarks for a statewide physician trade association. Physician burnout was a major common trend identified by all panelists. This topic created a beginning discussion leading to the association setting strategic goals for reaching out to early-career physicians, as well as developing wellness programs for doctors.

Second, your panelists will become more aware of your organization. They may become ambassadors for future collaboration and resources, creating a positive buzz about your organization. This can create huge wins for your organization.

Third, the expert panel will help bring an element of surprise and the value of learning something new for your attendees. They may share unedited, candid insight. I've found that this honest and straightforward input can pique the interest of even the most skeptical workshop participant. Your attendees may suddenly appreciate the opportunity to participate in their own strategic planning symposium. If attendees assume your meeting is just one more typical boring meeting, your opening panel often will prove them wrong!

For a nonprofit organization considering a capital campaign, I arranged a panel featuring a diverse group of fundraising consultants. Panelists were asked to share insight about the successes and pitfalls of launching a capital campaign. The nonprofit leaders were stunned at the level of preparation required.

I worked with a utility company whose executives wanted to learn about deregulation as part of their strategic plan workshop. I hosted an opening panel of company executives from telecommunications, transportation, and financial industries—sectors impacted by deregulation. Leaders shared deregulation survival lessons, mistakes, and victories. The deregulation panel made an impression, and the utility executives referred to these stories of predictable patterns and strikingly similar challenges throughout the remainder of their workshop.

Only once in my strategic planning career have I received the thumbs-down on creating an opening panel. The board chairman thought that it would take up too much workshop time and that participants would not learn anything new.

In this case, I relied on participants to bring their homework insights and become the "external trends" panel. This provided a brilliant deep-dive into external trends and competitors, thanks to their significant amount of pre-workshop analysis.

STEP 7: THINK ABOUT PRE-WORKSHOP HOMEWORK ASSIGNMENTS

You'll want to give some thought to a pre-workshop homework assignment for your participants. Homework analysis creates a platform for shared insight and strategy.

Work with your executive team to develop a general approach for pre-workshop homework. I recommend that you bring homework ideas to your first meeting with the top executive and team. Vet the ideas. With feedback, you can proceed to shape assignments and determine how to best communicate the assignments to all participants.

Assignments should be specific and achievable for each homework team. I prefer to set up teams with four to six participants in each. On the pages that follow, I share some of my favorite pre-workshop homework assignments. You'll find more in the appendix.

Or, create your own. Help your participants examine the external environment and consider how your organization's resources, skills, and competencies should be combined to create competitive advantage.

Even if you lead a small company or nonprofit, your pre-workshop homework can provide a profound opportunity for your executives to come to the strategic planning workshop prepared to change the trajectory of their organization. Consider the following large-company situation and how pre-workshop analysis could be scaled appropriately for your organization to reveal trends and new opportunities that hadn't been considered.

In 2019, retail giant Target launched a new small-format store strategy, after strategic planning analysis revealed that consumers were starting to prefer small marketplace shopping experiences rather than at crowded big-box retail environments. The small format test sites contributed more than $1 billion in total sales. Also as a result of tracking trends, that same year Target offered guests more ease and convenience with its programs "Drive Up" and "Order Pickup."

A year prior to COVID-19, Drive Up resulted in sales growth of more than 500 percent. Order Pickup resulted in sales growth of nearly 50 percent.[2] The following year, these services unexpectedly exploded in popularity during the international pandemic. While many retailers went out of business due to stay-at-home orders, Target thrived as an "essential service."

Target's forward-thinking retail developments began in strategy formation sessions well in advance of the pandemic. These strategies were the result of diligent trend monitoring and hours of market analysis prior to leadership discussions and executive decisions.

Your organization's pre-workshop homework adds a serious and fundamental component to your workshop—that is, engaging your participants with a pertinent assignment, and expecting them to show up ready to share external market insight. This part of the program is *not* to be taken lightly.

Interesting and important assignments may focus on topics such as competitive intelligence and best practices, SWOT analysis (strengths, weaknesses, opportunities, and threats for the organization), trends, and scenario-planning. Ideally, each team can focus on a different topic and be given 10 minutes to share highlights with a five-minute Q&A session.

Pros and Cons of SWOT

SWOT analysis was developed in the 1960s by management consultant Albert Humphrey at the Stanford Research Institute. Fortune 500 companies needed a more executable strategic planning methodology. Humphrey's Strengths–Weaknesses–Opportunities–Threats model provided a tangible way to put structure to strategic planning.

Today, many scholars believe that using the traditional SWOT analysis to describe the organization's current status creates a set of limiting factors that have the potential to paralyze creative thinking about the future.* Others argue that weaknesses or threats are management issues. They believe the focus should be put only on strengths and opportunities.

Yet other consultants believe that strategic plans have value only if they can serve as an overarching framework for the most important work of leadership, and that most critical is the development of nimble strategies to address emerging issues along with tactical plans for implementing those strategies.†

I'm a proponent for examining an organization through multiple lenses. I believe SWOT remains useful for focusing on strengths and opportunities as well as weaknesses and threats, if combined with competitive intelligence and other strategic planning team assessments noted in this book with emphasis on differentiated strengths and weaknesses compared to the competition. This reveals differentiated competitive advantages and disadvantages leading to insight and strategy choices.

While there are limitations in focusing only on the negative, I disagree that building only upon strengths provides sufficient insight for nimble, visionary strategic thinking. Leaders need to be sensibly aware and highly conscious of their organization's weaknesses and potential pitfalls. Then, and only then, will strategic opportunities become clear and compelling.

* Bauer 2017.
† LaPiana 2008.

In sum, pre-workshop homework creates executive learning, accountability, and commitment to the workshop because each participant is required to bring something of value to the table. As an added benefit, I've found that pre-workshop team assignments for completing important analysis can be one of the best ways to lighten the workload for you, or for the leader or consultant who curates the workshop.

PRE-WORKSHOP HOMEWORK TECHNIQUES

For your participants, pre-workshop homework adds executive skin in the game and promotes shared discovery. People support what they help to create. Ideally, you will share your homework assignment with the executive team a month prior to your scheduled strategic planning workshop and build the presentation into your meeting agenda. Participants will arrive to the workshop ready to share valuable homework insights, which will enhance teamwork. This strategic planning pre-meeting homework will help your organization increase personal ownership and allow specific participants to "own" a topic.

For you, the facilitator, the pre-meeting homework allows you to relax while each team contributes to the planning session. It reduces your investigative workload as the curator, shifting the work to those who will benefit from the knowledge over the long term.

Here are a few of my favorite, time-tested homework assignments.

SWOT Analysis

	STRENGTHS	WEAKNESSES
I N T E R N A L	• LIST IN BULLETS... SUCCINCT DESCRIPTIONS • LIST IN BULLETS... SUCCINCT DESCRIPTIONS • ETC...	• LIST IN BULLETS... SUCCINCT DESCRIPTIONS • LIST IN BULLETS... SUCCINCT DESCRIPTIONS • ETC...
	OPPORTUNITIES	**THREATS**
E X T E R N A L	• LIST IN BULLETS... SUCCINCT DESCRIPTIONS • LIST IN BULLETS... SUCCINCT DESCRIPTIONS • ETC...	• LIST IN BULLETS... SUCCINCT DESCRIPTIONS • LIST IN BULLETS... SUCCINCT DESCRIPTIONS • ETC...

Assign the SWOT Analysis to one or more teams to investigate the organization's strengths, weaknesses, opportunities, and threats. Use my SWOT analysis template as a helpful tool to capture your input. Team members can develop a brief report for each element and put findings into the SWOT template. Ask your homework team to share SWOT insights with the strategic planning workshop participants.

The SWOT analysis assignment should be completed prior to your strategic planning workshop. For example, it could be part of your executive homework assignment in one meeting or during a series of meetings. If your organization is small, you could create a SWOT dialogue as an all-employee activity, expanding pre-workshop analysis throughout an organization.

While the SWOT presentation is part of your strategic planning workshop, make an effort to keep it as brief as possible. The purpose of this exercise is to present SWOT findings, but it is not a problem-solving activity. It is simply a primer for the next activity.

After the SWOT highlights are shared, invite participants to contribute any additional input using my Quick Input Without Discussion technique noted here.

Quick Input Without Discussion

This technique is a great way to ask for further input during an exercise when you don't have time to discuss a topic any further. Ask the group to write additional input or ideas on Post-it notes and leave these either on the table at the end of the meeting, or on a blank flip chart posted on the wall.

This quick input can be summarized and added to your meeting notes without further discussion. This works well with SWOT discussions, after your internal team has presented the SWOT report and you're ready to move on. Quick Input also works anytime when you have a packed agenda and need to move on to other discussions.

Analysis Focused on Strengths

Finally, you can ask one or more pre-workshop homework teams to do a deep-dive analysis on "strengths as competitive advantage." For example, in California, a biotech start-up incubator focuses on providing what few other entrepreneur support groups provide: early-stage seed funding. The organization has built its investment process around vetting and awarding small-dollar investments for early-stage management teams who can prove that their company is addressing a unique marketplace need, has a solid management team structure, and can meet financial and other due diligence qualifications. The early-stage funding feature creates a sweet spot unduplicated by other investment groups in the region.

A private scholarship foundation in Colorado focuses on distributing funds to high school seniors who are active in and committed to participating in community service. While other college scholarships focus on academic grades and other criteria, this organization's distinct competitive advantage is focusing on high school students with proven track records of community service and a lifelong ambition of serving their communities.

Focusing on strengths will energize your strategic planning workshop. Especially for the nonprofit sector, this donor-focused question can reveal important insight for further discussion: What is our differentiating strength that makes us unique and helps us make the case that others should support our work?[3]

PESTEL Analysis

The PESTEL analysis is an easy assignment to assess your organization's external political, economic, sociocultural, technological, environmental, and legal factors. Questions could include: What factors are impacting our organization? Which are most important at this time? Which might become critically important in the next few years?

Competitive Intelligence

Competitive intelligence is activity within any organization to gather and analyze information about its industry, business environment, competitors, and competitive products and services. The information-gathering and analysis process can help a company develop its strategy and identify competitive gaps. Competitive intelligence can reveal risks and opportunities and enable faster reaction to competitors' actions and future events in the marketplace.

Competitive Intelligence Snapshot Tool

Understanding the competition is key to developing strategic goals to gain competitive advantage. Use the following chart to summarize your organization's competitors.

Add columns and rows as needed. This is an excellent executive homework assignment.

	YOUR COMPANY	COMPETITOR 1	COMPETITOR 2
Strategy			
Key asset			
Distinct advantage			
Top issues or nagging problems			
Grade or score the competition according to severity of threat. Develop a simple method for ranking the threat level, such as A–B–C.			

Digital Sphere Intelligence

What is your company's digital brand reputation?

Your organization's digital brand reputation includes your customers' perception of the brand, as well as comments posted by your constituents and stories written by the media.

As a pre-workshop assignment, ask one or more small teams to complete a digital competitive analysis scan. This should include assessing strengths and weaknesses of competitors' websites, social media presence, and other internet representation. Teams should review traditional platforms such as Instagram, Facebook, YouTube, and LinkedIn as well as new and emerging digital platforms.

While it's important to recognize that there are marketing companies for hire that can provide customized, more complex digital competitive analysis reports, your pre-workshop homework group still can provide a very useful assessment by using SWOT as the basic criteria.

For example, ask your team to assess each competitor's performance (at a high level) based on the strengths, weaknesses, opportunities, and threats of its digital presence. Based on the company's website and social media presence on various platforms, does the company's present and future performance appear to be strong, status quo, or weak?

Beyond a company's website, have teams go to competitors' job review sites such as Glassdoor and Indeed. What are current and former employees saying about the competitors?

Determine audience size for each social media platform. How many followers are on each profile? Assess each company's PR and marketing strategies. Which posts have the most engagement?

Have the team put together a brief presentation, and share it at the workshop. These visual presentations could feature social media and website screen snaps. Have each team make a few big-picture, strategic recommendations for enhancing your organization's digital presence.

As they report their findings, make sure they compare and contrast their observations with your organization. This includes online job reviews summarizing both the positive and negative comments about your organization. Teams could note any key words or descriptive phrases that create common themes.

———

Balanced Scorecard

A Balanced Scorecard is a performance metric used to measure and provide feedback to organizations. It is used in strategic management to identify and improve internal functions of a business and resulting external outcomes. The balanced scorecard was first introduced in 1992 in the *Harvard Business Review* by accounting academic Robert Kaplan and business executive and theorist David Norton.[4] There are many visual models of the Kaplan and Norton Balanced Scorecard available online.

For an excellent Balanced Scorecard homework assignment, you could ask your executive team or board members to break into teams and analyze customer survey results or other company data and develop answers to the four scorecard categories noted below.

1. How do customers see us?
   This is how your customers view your existing products and services.

2. What must we excel at?
   This is an internal perspective for quality and efficiency.

3. Can we continue to improve and create value?
   This is an organizational capacity, innovation, and learning perspective.

4. How do we look to shareholders?
   This is a financial performance perspective.

———

Jim Collins's *Good to Great* Questions

As a pre-workshop strategy activity to create understanding about an organization's competence and top drivers of your economic engine, have one or more teams answer the following three questions posed by Jim Collins in his *book Good to Great.*[5] Answers could be discussed and compared. Answers providing the most clarity and truth could be selected to define what products, services, and programs your organization can be best in the world at providing. Just as important, as Collins notes, this analysis can reveal what your organization *cannot* be best in the world at providing.

1. What is our organization—and our employees—deeply passionate about?
2. What can we, as an organization, be the best in the world at?
3. What drives our organization's economic engine?

––––––––

Michael E. Porter's Five Forces Analysis

Knowing who your competition is and assessing their programs, products, services, pricing, and marketing strategies is critical to determining how your organization can best compete. In Michael Porter's Five Forces model,[6] the five forces that shape industry competition include:

1. Competitive rivalry
2. The bargaining power of suppliers
3. The bargaining power of customers
4. The threat of new entrants
5. The threat of substitute products or services

A pre-workshop homework group could analyze your organization's top competitors and answer the following questions. A summarized report could be shared during the workshop.

Have one or more homework groups answer these questions:

1. What competition do we face in our industry?
2. What potential exists for new entrants into the industry?
3. What bargaining power or threats exist from suppliers?
4. What bargaining power or threats exist from customers?
5. What threats exist from potential substitute products?
6. And most important: What implications do these findings have for our organization's strategy?

The homework group's findings and potential recommendations for your organization will help support your strategic goal-setting session soon to follow.

———————

Scenario-Planning

Scenario-planning can provide a fun and interesting way to deal with the unforeseen and unplanned—for changes in the environment. Scenario-planning involves creating different possible futures, including multiple perspectives, based on how important trends might play out in a particular business setting and then testing the viability of your strategy in those worlds.[7] Many online tools are available to support scenario-planning activities; however, a skilled facilitator is advised to ensure that a range of scenario possibilities leads to flexible strategies, rather than betting the company on one sole scenario.

Scenario-planning does not lead to identifying a preferred scenario for the future. Rather, it focuses on the types of changes and new scenarios that are likely to occur, and what the organization can do to better prepare for unknown and unexpected situations. This builds personal and organizational resilience.

For example, your team could invent three to four different scenarios and assign a descriptive name for each. Teams would discuss the circumstances leading to each scenario, and then discuss the preparation needed to be ready for each situation.

As a senior administrator at Arizona State University, I served on a pandemic strategy planning task force more than ten years prior to the COVID-19 outbreak in 2020. Best-case, severe case, and worst-case pandemic scenarios were developed. Each featured a series of action steps.

At that time, these discussions seemed surreal. It was difficult to imagine how university events would be canceled, and how essential services such as housing and medical support would continue for students who could not return home. It was impossible to envision how classroom and administrative business would continue as people worked from home. After all, technology for remote meetings had not been invented just yet!

The task force scenario-planning created awareness and the ability to quickly mobilize when, just thirteen years later, COVID-19 hit. Our preparation undoubtedly created awareness, preparedness, and collaboration. This undoubtedly prepared ASU to mobilize swiftly in response to COVID-19. Within a week of state stay-at-home orders, all ASU courses were transitioned into virtual classes using Zoom. This was scenario-planning at its finest.

As part of your organization's pre-workshop analysis, you can lead a lively in-person or virtual scenario-planning meeting and bring summary results to your strategic planning workshop. Benefits of scenario-planning include developing focus and a nimble mindset about the organization's key issues, as well as potential goals and steps to mitigating future risk.

Follow these steps:

- First, define the issue, decision, question, or potential crisis to be discussed.

- Second, identify the driving forces or big shifts in society, economics, technology, and politics impacting that issue.

- Third, list uncertainties having a big impact on your organization.

- Fourth, identify four possible scenarios. Why four? Most planning consultants believe that with four scenarios, the exercise stays simple while also forcing the group to think beyond the standard three options that might otherwise be developed. Rather than try to predict the single, exact future that *will* occur, your group should consider a *range of four plausible futures* that could occur.

- As the fifth and final step, your team will discuss the various implications and impacts of each scenario. Discuss how your organization should respond to each scenario. Summarize and present findings at your strategic planning meeting.

It's important to note that complex scenario-planning may go beyond the capacity of a pre-workshop homework group conducting a simple brainstorm activity. Data-driven scenario-planning, such as predicting global unrest and economic modeling, may require experienced facilitators and analysts with skills needed for quantitative analysis and geopolitical intelligence. This goes well beyond the purview of our discussion here. I recommend a thorough search to discover scenario-planning firms based on your organization's needs and budget. In-depth analysis can reveal underlying trends of significance, along with future implications of emerging world events.

The American Planning Association and the Consortium for Scenario Planning partnered on the creation of the Scenario Planning KnowledgeBase,[8] a comprehensive web-based resource for practitioners interested in learning more about scenario-planning.

War-Gaming and Game Theory

War-gaming is a very specialized technique that visualizes the flow of a competitive battle, helping planners systematically consider the chain of events that occur as a unit of a particular course of action. War-gaming can reveal how competitors might respond to a company's strategies.[*] A summary of findings from pre-workshop war-gaming activities could be shared with strategic planning participants for the purpose of influencing goals.

Participants anticipate an opponent's moves from the opponent's point of view. This is a risk-free scenario game simulation in which moves are hypothetical only. By simulating a situation, a war game provides participants with experiential learning. War-gaming is a form of scenario-planning, and as a pre-workshop activity, it can be used to predict potential future competitor moves.

Game theory and "gamification" is an advanced analytical technique. However, due to its complexity, game theory may not be practical for smaller businesses and nonprofits because of the level of modeling and analytical software needed. The key here is to use the discipline to develop a range of outcomes based on decisions by reasonable actors and to present the advantages and disadvantages of each option.[†]

Following the pandemic planning, ASU created a war game to further test the task force's scenarios at Decision Theater, the university's interactive facility designed for game simulation. The pandemic exercise integrated a variety of disciplines and included artificial newscasts, electronic maps, charts, graphs, and up-to-the-minute health data compilation—including incomplete data. This allowed university administration to practice making decisions during a simulated pandemic.[‡] The convening of experts combined with analytics and predictive modeling allowed decision makers to understand the consequences of decisions before they were made.

* McNeilly 2014.
† McKinsey 2020.
‡ Robbins 2008.

Build a Strategic Plan Influencer Network

As part of the pre-meeting homework, assign a team to brainstorm a list of internal (employee) and external (constituent) influencers who could be invited to share your organization's strategic plan key messages through their social media networks. Keep in mind that external influencers could be categories based on your organization's important constituent groups, such as business leaders, key customers, donors, elected officials, or nonprofit leaders.

This homework assignment could be shared during the workshop to help jump-start your organization's communication plan, using social media as one strategy for promoting the strategic direction. The analysis also may reveal some of your organization's most powerful advocates.

STEP 8: DEPLOY IN-DEPTH PRE-WORKSHOP ANALYSIS

While pre-workshop homework provides in-depth analysis to be conducted by your strategic planning participants, ensuring their skin in the game, your organization may need a much deeper level of data collection, financial modeling, customer surveys, and market analysis requiring specific staff or consultant expertise and synthesis during the weeks or months prior to the strategic planning workshop.

You'll want to decide how this in-depth pre-workshop analysis will be communicated and accomplished. Valuable pre-workshop analysis could include activities organized by the organization's leaders, such as surveys and focus groups.

- **Conduct a formal, in-depth internal and external environmental scan.** Your organization could focus on completing a combination of the assessment tools noted in this book, including PESTEL, competitive intelligence, gap analysis, SWOT, strategic options/happy stories, and scenario-planning.

- **Conduct a customer/client/audience needs assessment, and summarize results.** This could include qualitative and quantitative research and data gathering, interviews with core and required partners, and inviting input from local stakeholders to identify service gaps.

- **Evaluate the organization's current board structure and capacity to support the strategic plan**. Analyze the board's skill background and recommend a framework to help the board implement the strategic plan. This type of analysis requires boldness and candor, with an agreement that with this board assessment, there is no sacred cow. A team of board members could be assigned to lead this assessment.

Focus Groups: Listening and Gathering

Ask your participants to conduct a customer, member, or specific constituent focus group. Focus groups can provide valuable opportunities to listen to your stakeholders and understand their expectations, wants, and needs. The groups can include employees, customers, donors, volunteers, communities, neighborhoods, or any specific group important to your organization fulfilling its mission.

For example, for leaders wanting to know more about how customers view their organization's products, focus group questions could include the following:[9]

1. Today's topic is [your product]. What are your general feelings about it?

2. What do you already know about this product? What is something more you would like to learn about it?

3. How did you first hear about this product?

4. What words or phrases come to mind when you think of this product?

5. How familiar are you with this product?

6. When, how, and where do you use this product?

7. What do you like best about this specific product?

8. What are your problems or concerns when using this product?

Focus group questions will be shaped to seek relevant marketing information needed to help your leaders develop strategic goals. When creating focus group questions, it's helpful to warm up group discussion by starting simple and progressing to more complex questions as the conversation flows.

Observations gleaned from focus group discussion should be summarized and presented as part of your strategic planning introductory analysis. (All pre-workshop analysis should be shared prior to the strategy-shaping, as a precursor to the intense strategic goal discussion to follow.)

For example, a nonprofit, volunteer-led artist association invited members to participate in focus groups to learn why memberships had dropped to an all-time low. The reason became clear: the individual artists expressed that they were angry that the organization had not supported their businesses with marketing services.

The board was shocked to learn about this confusion. The organization was established for only one reason—to promote and host an annual art walk. It was never intended to provide year-round marketing for individual businesses. This is why artists felt they were not receiving value for their membership dues.

This insight was brought to the board's strategic planning meeting. The board developed several key strategic "recovery" goals. A goal was developed to clarify the organization's purpose and brand. Another goal focused on creating new member marketing value in efforts to regain and grow membership. These goals were aimed specifically to support the organization's crumbling Financial and External Outreach pillars. With focus and a lot of outreach, within twelve months—year one of the three-year strategic plan—the board was able to restore communication with most of the lapsed members, manage their membership expectations, regain trust, and grow membership by 10 percent.

————

STEP 9: SECURE COMMITMENT TO A GOAL-TRACKING SYSTEM

Once your strategic plan is shaped, your organization will need to monitor ongoing progress toward its goals. You will want to ensure that your executive team is committed to instituting a meaningful goal measurement system (or dashboard) to track and cascade goals to all levels of the organization. You will also want to help your executive team understand that strategic planning is a vital, *ongoing process* requiring ongoing communication—not a one-and-done event.

All employees must understand how their work aligns with and supports the organization's success. However, this first meeting is not the time to discuss a specific tracking solution, as this will merit a dedicated conversation including discussion about tracking options. Ideally, decisions about an effective tracking system should be discussed early on during the workshop planning process, to budget and plan for introducing the new system.

However, during this early discussion with the executive team, do seek and secure the team's commitment to select a tracking system, as well as to communicate and celebrate strategic plan results. Specifics will come later.

STEP 10: CONCLUDE WITH ANY OTHER IMPORTANT QUESTIONS ABOUT LOGISTICS

You will want to discuss other important issues with your executive team. Some of these could include the following:

- Who will facilitate our meetings? Unless the executive team has a strong recommendation about who should facilitate, you may be in the best position to select a capable facilitator, or *you* may be best suited to serve in this role.

- What should we *call* our strategic planning sessions? Workshop? Summit? Conference? Strategic conversations? What communicates value and the serious worth to be received by both the organization as a whole and each attendee?

- Will there be a theme to support the effort? My favorite strategic planning themes are brief and connote big ideas, urgency, inclusiveness, diversity of participants (age, ethnicity, geographic location, professional background, and expertise), and the idea of boundary spanning—bringing people together from all departments and divisions of a company. When you research business-meeting themes online, you'll find plenty of inspiring theme ideas:

- An Invitation to Innovate

- World of Opportunities

- It Starts with Us

- ReImagine

- Next Level

- Reaching New Heights Together

- Mastermind Summit

Any vivid theme that points to the future could be designed into an eye-catching invitation and delivered or e-mailed personally to each invited participant. What descriptions work well for the organization? These must be words, phrases, or concepts that have potential to create gravitas and intrigue. Taking it to the next level of surprise, you could put the invitation in a box with a small gift, fun party favor, or treat to support the theme.

I helped an organization develop a series of planning meetings called "The Puzzle Forum." The theme communicated that each person's voice was an important contribution, similar to puzzle pieces coming together to form a complete picture. Each invitee received a large puzzle piece featuring a part of the company's logo along with their invitation. This piqued interest, and all of the invitees showed up.

———

A CONSULTANT'S WORKSHEET FOR STEP 1

Help Your Executive Team Set Strategic Planning Program Goals for the Workshop, Written Plan, and Tracking and Communication Systems

When you meet with your executive team, here are some questions you can ask to ensure that each part of your strategic planning framework leads to desired outcomes as articulated by the executive team ultimately accountable for achieving results.

Workshop Questions

1. What is the single most important outcome that you think we need to achieve in order to create a meaningful strategic planning workshop experience or process? Some workshop outcome examples could include:

   - Bond with our board of directors, staff, and invited constituents.
   - Work at a strategic level across all departments, eliminating company silos.
   - Develop a bold new direction to excel and grow internationally.
   - Sharpen external trend and issue awareness.
   - Understand our organization's strengths, weaknesses, opportunities, and threats (SWOT).
   - Create a company-wide learning mindset and bold new competitive possibilities.
   - Ensure company-wide alignment and buy-in for strategic objectives.
   - Enhance board of director leadership engagement and sense of duty to the organization.

- Survey members to understand program needs and new opportunities for the organization.

2. What *one* type of activity would you include to make the strategic planning experience more engaging, insightful, and successful? Such activities could feature guest speakers with dialogue, breakout sessions to discuss current company issues, and topics focused on company culture.

3. How might we include external constituents (such as customers, donors, elected officials, suppliers, strategic collaborating partners) who could add valuable insight impacting our future? Challenge insular thinking. Instead of relying only on ideas from leaders within your organization, help your executive team see the value of including strategic input from external constituents where outside perspectives could provide a fresh perspective. Input could focus on customer service, branding, and marketing topics.

You can create opportunities where external input can be injected into your strategic planning workshop. For example, your organization could include an opening panel featuring external speakers, followed by a summary sharing customer survey results. Or, your company could host a lunch presentation and dialogue during your strategic planning workshop, where constituents are invited to attend lunch and hear a guest speaker or strategic presentation followed by the opportunity to address table topics or a series of planned questions in smaller groups.

Written Plan Questions

The written strategic plan *is* the story of your organization's overall strategic intent, and it describes your future. This written strategy document will provide the foundation for speeches, newsletter articles, social media posts, and progress reports. It's the concrete product or outcome of your workshop. Work with your executive team and ask some important questions like these:

1. What are your goals for the written plan? Some written plan goal examples could include the following:

   - To create a flexible three-year strategic plan that helps the organization grow its capacity to meet customer (member, constituent) needs and priorities.
   - Clearly describe the organization's strategic pillars—and communicate the strategic goals supporting each pillar.
   - Develop growth strategies for our organization's national or global scale-up.
   - Focus company resources and staff energy.
   - Develop strategies for community-building, movement-building, and mission advocacy.
   - Produce a digital infographic that provides a visual overview of the written strategic plan for sharing internally as well as with external constituents.

2. What's the desired timing for completing the written strategic plan, and for kicking off the program?

3. How do you envision the written plan will be launched and communicated? Will there be a series of meetings with employees? Will the plan be available to employees through online (intranet) publication?

Tracking and Communication System Questions

1. What system for tracking makes most sense for your organization? That is, do you have a recommendation for a system of tracking? If the executive team has operated without a goal-tracking system, they may not have an answer. If so, offer to provide options for

goal tracking at a future meeting. This could include a goal-tracking demonstration within online, cloud-based programs.

2. How frequently will the strategic plan be tracked and progress reported?

3. How can we engage the human resources team so that strategic plan metrics are linked to department and individual performance?

4. How can we engage the communication staff as part of the strategic plan management team to ensure timely internal and external progress bulletins and goal accomplishments?

5. What are your goals for your tracking plan? Here are some examples of strategic plan tracking goals:

   - Track and report goal progress for each quarter.
   - Show how all departments are contributing to enterprise-level progress.
   - Develop a meaningful goal cascading system connecting employee, department, and enterprise-level goals.
   - Create a visual diagram clearly showing how all departments and staff members are contributing to the company's strategic plan.

Again, don't be surprised if the executive team has not considered how the tracking and communication system will be evaluated and selected. You can recommend meeting with the team again to bring solutions and discuss options for an appropriate tracking system that can be implemented within budget and ongoing schedule.

CHAPTER 3

YOUR VITAL WORKSHOP: A LIFE-CHANGING, SHARED EXPERIENCE

THE WORKSHOP PART OF MY STRATEGIC planning equation is, from my experience, the most important part of the entire strategic planning process. Your workshop will be an irreplaceable investment of time, insight, and strategy development. When participants learn from each other—and find value in the experience—the energy and momentum you generate here will set your organization in motion for years to come.

If you want vital, life-changing strategic planning, then you have to create a participative, shared, and meaningful workshop that is itself life changing. A life-changing strategic planning workshop can strengthen internal social capital, your leadership team's foundation of authentic community. The word "authentic" is derived from the Greek definition of "one who accomplishes." Authenticity in the context of community building and social capital is inclusive, is self-correcting for actions taken, requires empowerment and action, sets direction, and is grounded in ethics.

Human connectivity translates into a culture of enhanced trust and support for the strategic direction, starting with the leadership team and cascading throughout your organization.

Whether you call it a workshop, a retreat, a symposium, or any other name—and whether it's a one-day event or conducted as a series of events—you, as a leader in charge of your organization's strategic plan (whether you are the CEO, a planning executive, consultant, facilitator, or a board member) have the power (and responsibility) to create strategic momentum for your organization. In the process, your strategic planning workshop can play an important role in creating and nurturing trusted friendships.

Your organization is a system that exceeds the sum of its parts. Your workshop will activate your team's "systems thinking" ability—the ability to see that everything is connected. The workshop may inspire curiosity, openness, and resilience. It may help your team navigate complexity and grow tolerance for ambiguity. It may expand participants' analytical ability, as well as interpersonal and communication skills.

During the Great Recession of 2008, a colleague of mine who is a busy architect and senior leader of a 1,500-member global architecture and design firm built an engaging strategic planning experience for his company at a time when many firms faced a prolific stall of projects. Selected for his deep industry knowledge and trusted reputation, he confided, "We had no survival strategy. I started our first strategic planning meeting by asking my leaders for big ideas about what differentiated us in the marketplace. I pressed them hard to articulate what was unique about our company that no one else could claim."

Three core values emerged: "Designs that inspire, connect, and perform." Inspire, connect, and perform defined the ethos for the company's projects, such as airports that connect a variety of terminals, retail, and main spaces and "perform" by supporting operations, while creating inspirational spaces people enjoy while traveling.

From there, my colleague and his planning team fanned out across the globe and met with employee groups. His team created a ground-up focus group approach to search for further answers to the competitive advantage question. Exploration, research, and discovery were additional values distinct to his firm's ability to deliver extraordinary designs. Then, the team turned their attention to developing three-year strategic goals and a system for tracking and communicating results. Work groups were reorganized to focus on achieving the strategic goals. Unlike many architecture and design firms during that traumatic slowdown, his company made a profit. The firm was fortunate to have had a leader who took the creative strategic planning approach of appreciative inquiry, which was a perfect fit for this particular organization. He focused attention on the organization's strengths and competitive advantage, with a core premise that everyone's ideas count.

A LIFE-CHANGING WORKSHOP IS . . .

An investment in building internal social capital

Relationships matter. Your organization's leadership team represents a compilation of valuable networks, resources, and associations that can be mobilized to achieve competitive advantage and strategic impact. Your organization's strategic planning workshop can strengthen the durability of internal relationships. This aggregated social capital drives information exchange, decision making, and collective action.

Custom Crafted

If you want to create a meaningful, life-changing workshop experience for an organization and its members, you'll need to custom craft it to fit the organization's needs and culture. When you take it upon yourself to curate your shared experience with care, each member of the strategic planning team will feel valued. And they will be confident that their investment of time will result in strategic impact.

Anticipated

It's important to create anticipation for your workshop experience. To do this, you'll want to kick off the anticipation of strategic planning *weeks prior* to the actual event. Your invitation should create excitement, intrigue, and gravitas. It should prompt a sense of responsibility to arrive prepared and ready to participate. An eye-catching event invitation can add an element of fun, as well as affirm the importance of each individual participant having a seat at the table.

Some of my favorite strategic planning invitations are simple but powerful, such as:

The (Company Name)
Management Team
Invites you to

THE BIG CONVERSATION

A Strategic Planning Summit to create a
distinctive, inclusive, connected, and vibrant future
for (organization's name here).

You're Invited!

VISION

For our Future
(You bring the dreams, we'll provide the
food | drinks | dialogue starters.)

The mayor invites you to a

VISIONING LAB

To create our community's future.

As old-fashioned as it seems, people still enjoy receiving eye-catching paper invitations, whether sent to their home (with more people working from home these days) or personally placed on desks or in their office mailboxes. A personalized, spectacular hard copy or digital invitation will feature an interesting subject line, such as the workshop theme.

Personalize each invitation. Include a message from your organization's top executive. Describe the purpose and expected outcomes from the workshop. Note the meeting date, time, and location, and any required preparation such as pre-workshop homework. You could provide a website link to the planned agenda.

Realistic

This chapter provides an effective strategic planning agenda framework you can customize. Make sure the time required is realistic for staff, board, and guest participants. Ask the executive team to reserve their calendars for all scheduled dates and times.

Adaptable

Advise your executive team that they'll benefit by being flexible and anticipating the possibility of a few scheduling surprises during the workshop. A speaker may fail to show up, a discussion may become heated, or a conversation may run over the allotted time. Assure the leadership team that you'll reroute the agenda as needed.

Entertaining

Everyone enjoys hospitality. And yes, we want to be entertained. As soon as participants enter your strategic planning workshop, they should feel welcome. We appreciate being pampered and hosted, especially when we take time from our packed schedules to spend a day or more away from work. Hospitality will set your strategic planning workshop apart from routine meetings.

Curated By You

You, the strategic planning curator, are the life changer. You are creating the time and space for leaders—human beings—to come together and feel heard, respected, and valued. You're helping the organization's leadership team curate—that is, choose, organize, and thoughtfully present each workshop activity for the sole purpose and outcome of developing strategies leading to strategic goals, which then will be further broken into annual, twelve-month goals.

Never underestimate the inspiration created by your strategic planning workshop, and you as the curator. As people arrive with their own sets of priorities and problems, your leadership will create important human connections and a unified focus to drive strategic thinking. You are essential for helping the executive team invent your organization's future.

While the pre-workshop preparation may feel a lot like special event planning, the truth is that it *does* take significant foresight to help your organization conceive and implement a life-changing strategic planning workshop—one that blends strategy shaping with discovery and fun. In this chapter, I offer many pre-workshop ideas that have worked well with my clients—recommendations to help you think of things that might not occur as you guide your organization. This leads to a robust and flexible strategic planning workshop framework that you can customize and make your own.

WE WANT OUR WORK TO MATTER

In today's work environment, whether we work at an organization's office or work outside the boundaries of a physical location in a distributed environment such as our home or a coffee shop, we want our work to count and to contribute to a great cause. We also want to be included and feel engaged in the organization's future, and we want to contribute to that future by getting important things done. We don't want to waste time. According to Simpplr and Glassdoor research, employees want to know how their work and their company can make a positive impact. Employees want to be aligned with strategic priorities, and they want to participate in a culture where they feel safe, connected, and supported.[1]

Exceptional strategic planning and conscientious implementation of the plan can enhance employee engagement by creating purpose, alignment, and community. That's why your strategic planning workshop experience is so important. It's the first step of a vital, three-part framework.

When Strategic Planning Team Members Feel Valued

- Each team member's strengths and contributions are appreciated by the group.

- One team member says to another, "Great idea. I'll support that."

- Conflicting priorities are transformed into several top strategic priorities and long-term opportunities.

- A skeptical team member turns from negative to positive in support of the strategic direction.

- Leaders see a new vision and get excited about the organization's strategic future.

WE THRIVE IN AN ENVIRONMENT OF TRUST WHERE SILOS ARE ELIMINATED

Strategic planning can foster vital moments of bonding when team members are inspired by their organization's story, including its past, present, and future. Help your leadership team create goals and shared expectations for the strategic planning workshop. This includes the opportunity to be heard, to contribute insight, to problem solve, and to dream big.

An effective strategic planning facilitator can help leadership teams conquer a history of silos and underlying distrust.

A bank executive was invited to facilitate a strategic planning meeting for the parent company. The opening exercise was instrumental in dissolving a long history of executive peer distrust.

"I asked each executive to turn to the next colleague. Each leader was charged with pairing up and taking two minutes to introduce themselves," she later recalled. When time was up, each executive was required to introduce his or her discussion partner based on that person's strengths. The exercise required each executive to hit the reset button—and see the best in another leader who might have been a personal rival.

"It was a humbling experience," she noted. "There were tears as emotional stories were shared. This set a productive tone for the remainder of the strategic planning workshop. We were able to work together in unity and support of each other, with no finger pointing or pontification."

Team trust is essential, impacting the pinnacle of your strategic planning program, the strategic goal-setting process. When team trust exists and silos are eliminated, there's plenty of room for group input, instead of wordsmithing or arguing about minutiae. Following the strategic planning workshop, the organization's staff or executive team can dedicate more time to fine-tune each pillar's goals.

YOUR WORKSHOP ALSO HAS PRACTICAL NEEDS

A brilliant strategic planning workshop is exceptionally curated: that is, content is thoughtfully selected, customized to fit your organization, and presented for the purpose of developing strategic goals leading to your organization's written strategic plan—the shared story of strategic intent. A well-curated workshop can be hosted in one to two days with intense preparation.[2] That's good news for smaller organizations and tiny start-ups where time is scarce. Larger companies may prefer a slower, more staged, or deliberate procedure through a scheduled series of meetings.

I believe that strategic planning typically should not drag on for more than six months, unless there's a clear end point and a series of specific milestones communicated up front. I've found that dedicated strategic planning work spaces can provide focus and a heightened sense of mission. This can be especially helpful for long strategic planning processes.

For example, I worked many months with the executive management team at a large technology company. They requested a series of meetings focused on examining competitive intelligence and scenario-planning. Each meeting required many hours of analysis in preparation for discussions. An ad-hoc work group was assigned, working furiously between strategic planning workshop sessions. To add gravitas and focus to this endeavor, the CEO dedicated a "pop-up" war room to the work group. A large conference room was staged for interactive conversations and whiteboard discussions. The physical transformation of a conference room to "war room" generated excitement, and to this day, I'm convinced that it enhanced thought leadership as well as analysis. The sheer act of creating a dedicated space clearly communicated the CEO's commitment to the company's planning process.

Don't Skimp on Hiring an Effective Strategic Planning Consultant

If you are a leader within an organization and are charged with hiring an outside strategic planning consultant who guides the process (which may or may not be the meeting facilitator), interview more than one to find the right fit. Select someone whose personality, leadership style, and planning approach are well matched to your organization's culture.

If your organization is a large law firm with multiple offices, the firm's traditional corporate culture will require a facilitator whose personality matches the attorneys and who is seen as a credible facilitator—possibly someone with a law degree. If your organization is a university, a professor with business and strategic planning expertise could provide a good match for those in academia. Similar backgrounds can be helpful, but this is not the most important determinant of an effective facilitator. In fact, some executives note that industry experience can work *against* strategic planning consultants when they try to steer the process to what they think they know best. I believe the two most important factors for selecting an effective strategic planning consultant include:

- Selecting an experienced leader and strategic planning expert who has worked in a variety of industry sectors, and who has assisted similar-size organizations develop strategic goals to address *similar challenges*; and

- A personality, pace, and consultative style that works well with the firm's culture and executive team personalities. I've seen expressive and jovial personalities work well with certain cultures such as arts, hospitality, and behavioral health organizations, while the same humor may not work quite as well with the corporate cultures of banking and accounting.

Your strategic planning consultant should be able and willing to become immersed in your organization's history, culture, key issues, and past successes.

If you are the executive director of a small nonprofit, budget limitations may prevent your organization from hiring a strategic planning consultant. Try finding a local business willing to provide a loaned executive to provide assistance.

If you're the consultant assisting with the strategic plan, more than likely you will be the facilitator for the workshop. However, it is not uncommon for the company to provide facilitation tag-team support for particular activities, giving you a break in the action. Perhaps one of your board members has strategic planning expertise and is willing to forgo being a workshop participant to assist in facilitating some of the discussions. This can provide speaker variety and credibility, similar to an engaging newscast featuring several expert reporters.

Select a Great Facilitator (If You Are Not Facilitating)

An effective facilitator makes *all* the difference. My worst memory of the wrong facilitator was at a nonprofit strategic planning workshop in a fancy hotel conference center, where a well-meaning facilitator began the meeting on the wrong foot. He opened the workshop with an exercise to revise the organization's vision. The facilitator made the classic mistake of developing an agenda *without input from the board*.

This forty-year-old organization did *not* need to have its vision statement changed, and the facilitator, unfortunately, was not experienced with handling conflict. Within the first five minutes, a heated conversation ensued. It reached the boiling point when an upset board member threw a fork across the room, nearly stabbing another board member in the face. Moments later, the volatile board member apologized, the group took a break, and the rest of the day was awkward. As the discussion heated up, an experienced facilitator would have taken immediate steps to pull the group together, seek clarity for the half-day retreat, and help the board move beyond the emotional outbursts.

Tag-Team the Facilitation

Sometimes it's great to invite a tag-team facilitator to join you at the podium, to interject expertise and information during your presentation, and then to help you move around the room to collect input.

However, for small breakout groups such as the pillar discussions where the Fail-Succeed exercise is used as well as the hot-topic discussions, preappoint and train breakout facilitators so they are prepared to lead small-group breakout discussions. Make sure each group facilitator understands his or her role and the purpose of the breakout discussion. Whether you conduct the breakouts in separate rooms near the main room or whether you congregate small groups in corners or at big wall spaces of a large room, appoint a facilitator for each breakout group to keep the topical conversations on point.

Keep Things Moving, and Encourage 100 Percent Participation

An effective facilitator knows how to keep discussions moving forward. If you are the facilitator, you'll need to actively manage group discussions to avoid having any one person derail the conversation or hog the floor. Ensure that all voices are heard. Point to someone who has not spoken up and say: We haven't heard from you yet—what are your thoughts about the topic?

To ensure all voices are heard, I like to ask: Does anyone have a different point of view? I'm delighted when I see a hand go up. That's when I know I've empowered someone to either disagree or share a different perspective.

More about Hiring a Strategic Planning Consultant

- Hire a great strategic planning consultant who might also be the facilitator.

Don't be like the firm who hired a $300,000 consultant and after many unproductive meetings, the company was in chaos and there was still no strategic plan. If your organization needs to hire a consultant or firm to help you plan your strategic planning program, select an experienced strategic planner with a verified track record of delivering effective workshops, written plans, and tracking systems. Check their references.

All workshop activities recommended by the facilitator or consultant (whether it is you or you hire someone) should be vetted and have executive or steering committee support. Typically, the CEO or most senior planning executive serves as the company's strategic planning decision maker and point person for you, the strategic planning consultant. If this is not the case, your organization's top executive can appoint a trusted internal liaison to provide periodic checkpoints for all decisions pertaining to your company's strategic planning process.

- Determine the best roles for your organization's staff, versus the consultant's responsibilities.

For example, your staff may be most useful in researching industry trends and competitive intelligence. Your consultant might be best for structuring your strategic planning meetings, facilitating workshops, and writing your strategic plan first draft. A consultant might serve as sounding board for the CEO and serve as a trusted advisor for helping you develop next steps, including tracking results.

- Be sure your consultant's service contract clearly spells out all deliverables and outcomes.

An effective strategic planning facilitator completes an extraordinary amount of homework. If you hire a facilitator, be sure to monitor results and provide feedback to your consultant after each planning session.

- If you are considering hiring a strategic planning expert or planning firm, look for a solution provider who fits well with your firm's culture. Your candidate should have a track record for delivering both a result-oriented strategic plan as well as developing a process that helps you build greater teamwork and participant engagement. The workshop planning process is just as important as the final product!

- If you or your company has hired a strategic planning consultant, either directly oversee your consultant's work or assign someone from your team to be the go-to source for all decisions associated with your company's strategic planning process. Make sure that all activities recommended by your consultant have executive management's full support. Be sure that the service contract for your consultant clearly reflects your company's expectations for the strategic planning process as well as planning outcomes. Monitor results and provide feedback to your consultant after each planning session.

Tips for Hiring an Effective Meeting Facilitator (Facilitator Only)

- Hire a strategic planning facilitator who communicates well with your organization's leadership team, board, and culture. For example, hire someone who is skilled at developing good group conversations, keeping the agenda on track, and managing potential conflicts.

- Hire a skilled facilitator who fits well with your firm's culture.

For example, if your company culture is firm and fast-paced, select a facilitator who is direct and keeps the conversation moving. If your organization's culture is highly discussion oriented, your facilitator should be masterful at soliciting robust feedback, inviting those who

continued

are more reserved to share opinions and preventing those more vocal from dominating conversations.

- Ensure that your facilitator is a strong meeting leader, but not arrogant—someone who is objective and neutral who also can develop vital conversations and seek contributions from each participant.

An Expert Facilitator Helps Everyone Know Their Input Is Important

Good listening and communication skills are at the core of good facilitation. When your facilitator (you or someone else) is a good and patient communicator, it helps build trust and openness in the group. When people understand each other, they make better decisions. In addition to listening, your facilitator should be able to inject humor into the conversation when appropriate and laugh with the group, lighten things up when needed, and take nothing personally. Skills a competent communicator will use are:

- Active listening that enables all participants to hear what others are saying.

- Questioning that helps clarify what people are saying, or supports people to explore their needs and come up with new possibilities.

- Summarizing that helps remind participants of the key points in the discussion and check that they have the same understanding.

- Synthesizing that allows the group to bring together different views and ideas to form one proposal that works for everyone.

PRE-WORKSHOP CHECKLIST

Seek Steering Committee Guidance

A leadership steering committee can help you avoid land mines and garner a strong circle of support for your strategic planning process. Land mines can include company politics and hidden agendas, where it's good to know pertinent backstories and strong opinions that may exist under the surface as hidden roadblocks among your strategic planning participants.

For example, a strategic planning leader was ready to invite a guest speaker to participate in the opening panel. The speaker was a prominent thought leader in a relevant industry. After speaking with a steering committee member, it was revealed that this potential speaker was currently in a lawsuit with the leader's organization! This bit of insight averted an embarrassing situation for both the strategic planning leader and her organization.

In certain milieus such as medicine, research, and academia, credentials *do* count. Strong opinions may exist regarding who is taken seriously as a panelist, for example, and who is not.

Create a critical mass of trusted advisors who support the strategic planning agenda. Invite the company's top executive to appoint a strategic planning steering committee. Steering committees can help you vet panel speakers and hot-topic breakout participants to ensure credibility with your organization. Steering committees also can help you ensure an inclusive, diverse strategic planning program that invites voices from all age, ethnic, geographic, and skill backgrounds representing your organization and its external constituents. Diverse viewpoints enhance the variety of input that is helpful in keeping the agenda on-track.

Once you and your CEO have agreed upon a planning schedule and draft agenda, vet the plan with your steering committee, and adjust as needed.

Hire or Assign a Meeting Scribe for Note-Taking

Before the strategic planning workshop, I highly recommend that you assign or hire a trusted writer to scribe detailed, accurate notes of all workshop presentations and discussions. Your scribe will save you hours of recap work later. Your scribe can help you ensure a more accurate workshop summary while you focus on the workshop content, discussion, and room dynamics.

You or your expert writer will use the workshop summary to shape your organization's written strategic plan. After the meeting, I recommend that you and your writer prepare a few at-a-glance tables or summary grids so that you can simplify intricate analysis and help readers extrapolate the key findings.

Not all workshop activity summaries will go into the main body of your written strategic plan. However, you can choose to put certain notes, such as detailed pre-meeting homework reports, in the appendix. This works well for items such as the SWOT analysis and competitive intelligence summaries.

Confidential and proprietary workshop notes not suitable for the published strategic plan should be saved in your organization's files rather than included in the final plan.

Create Buzz

All strategic planning leaders face the same challenge: *How can I build workshop momentum from the moment participants walk into the room?* In reality, if you want excitement, you will have started turning the flywheel months before your workshop day. For some participants, the burden of time spent at a strategic planning workshop can seem like a heavy weight if they feel they need to be working on personal deadlines. At any given moment, a number of things are competing for their time and attention.

The executive team's message should convey urgency and importance for the strategic planning workshop, while also inspiring participants that they will be attending something special—similar to an interactive symposium where attendees will learn and grow professionally.

Creating pre-workshop excitement will help your workshop participants rise above the distractions and alternate pressures, and is one of the most significant ways to ensure your participants arrive to your workshop ready for a valuable, productive experience in which they will devote all their attention.

The best way to do this is by providing a sneak peek at the workshop's significant content. You can reveal the topics and guest speakers who will offer novel ideas. You can show how lively discussions focused on business problems and new vision will be woven in throughout the workshop.

Another way to create anticipation for an exceptional strategic planning shared experience is by sending a clever invitation a few weeks prior to the workshop to all participants. An eye-catching invitation can be as simple or elaborate as your budget allows. This provides a sneak peek at the significant workshop content. Making your presentation unique is an advantage, as it sets the tone for everything that follows.

One of my favorite workshop invitations arrived with a hockey puck inserted into a clear plastic envelope. Designed to create an irresistible urge to open it right away, this stunning package was hand-delivered to each participant's office. It featured the famous quote by hockey player Wayne Gretzky: "Skate to where the puck is going, not where it has been." The planning meeting was held at a National Hockey League arena. On the invitation, the host city's mayor was noted as the keynote speaker.

As a result, the attendance response rate for this planning workshop was 100 percent. I was amazed to see how our invitation created an extra spark of energy. The workshop started with an upbeat tone, similar to a sports pep rally!

Another memorable invitation riffed on a 1960s comedy television show, *Get Smart*. This popular show featured secret agents (Agent 86 and Agent 99) with well-known catchphrases including "Would you believe . . . ", "Missed it by that much," "Sorry about that, Chief," and "I asked you not to tell me that."

My organization's strategic planning workshop theme was "Get Smarter." This theme emphasized competitive intelligence, examining future trends, and setting strategy. Each attendee received an invitation placed in a small box designed with the show's iconic actors and famous lines. This created expectation for a fun retreat. The workshop opened with a surprise skit starring several of the managers. The skit ended with Agent 86 making a call on a replica of the show's renowned shoe phone, welcoming the CEO to the stage. The pre-workshop promotion and opening act demonstrated the organization's commitment to creating a fun and productive leadership experience.

Maximize your power to create buzz for your workshop. Everything you do, from the invitations to other pre-workshop materials, including pre-workshop homework, a special invitation delivered or e-mailed to participants, and pre-event promotional gifts, such as a logoed ball cap, will make for strong anticipation for your workshop—and ensure it will then live on in the participants' minds.

More Ways to Create Interest

You want your participants to walk into your workshop feeling honored to participate. And they should leave the meeting with a greater sense of pride and purpose for their organization. You can help the executive team foster gravitas for the strategic planning workshop by using a few of the ideas that follow.

- Have your CEO issue an eye-catching paper (hard copy) invitation, digital invitation, or both—to be hand-delivered or strategically e-mailed to the invited participants.

- For pre-meeting promotion, offer a promotional gift if the budget allows, such as a coupon created especially to promote something fun to be offered at the workshop—sunglasses, mystery gift boxes, or a gift that supports your meeting theme.

Provide digital gift bags for attendees. First, create a landing web page set up on your organization's website to promote your strategic planning workshop. The landing page could include workshop announcements, homework assignments, and a digital gift bag created especially for strategic planning participants. A digital gift bag is an innovative way to build participants' expectations for a high-quality, fun workshop, whether hosted in person or as a virtual program. Your landing page can offer an ability to click on a gift option, such as a company-branded T-shirt or reusable water bottle. The gift item could be shipped to each participant (the logistics of the gift store could be arranged by an assigned staff member or vendor). You could offer a prize for answering a strategic question. You also could provide special offers from sponsors, such as free webinars and e-books. This would require someone to manage the online promotion setup.

- Video is a popular way to present information, especially in a short format. Use video as a teaser to promote your strategic planning topics, speakers, and workshop venue. Feature leaders' sound bites to pique interest and pose questions to be addressed.

- Do whatever you can to ensure that your meeting invitation communicates significance and an honor to be invited. These ideas represent the tip of the iceberg.

- Provide a unique welcome gift for all your workshop participants. Think about your company and make the gift one they will remember. This can be a gift branded with your organization's logo (or not)—small in size but useful, and something each person will appreciate, such as luggage tags, a journal book, travel neck pillow, blue-light glasses, reusable steel water bottle, travel coffee mug, or portable phone charger. Give the gift to each person either as they arrive or place the gifts at each table setting.

- If you don't really have the budget for a gift, invite a partnering company—such as a supplier to the organization, banker, or corporate law firm—to "sponsor" a promotional gift, or ask an author to provide complementary books. Or you can print an interesting article related to an important topic, roll it up, pair it with a pen or other useful item, and tie them both up with a ribbon or cord. Even if your organization's gift is simple, it doesn't mean it won't go a long way toward creating a special experience where participants feel valued. People remember when they see that care has been put into an effort. You'll be enhancing your own reputation at the same time you are providing others with token of your appreciation of their time.

- On the final workshop day, as a meeting closer, ask your participants to share something they learned or a valuable insight that they had. This will not only reinforce what you discussed and bring to light what some participants may have missed, but it will also give participants a personal insight into their fellow participants. This will close your meeting, giving participants a sense of affirmation that they spent their time wisely. This is another positive reflection on you, the vital strategic planning expert.

Select the Perfect Workshop Location

The "perfect" workshop location doesn't need to be fancy or expensive. However, the venue needs to create a cheerful, productive, and collaborative environment for your group. No one wants to be shut up in a room that feels dark, dusty, or claustrophobic. Do your homework and take time to find the right place.

If you're stumped for ideas, check with your city's chamber of commerce, economic development, or hotel and hospitality industry association, as well as nonprofit trade associations and collaborative organizations with meeting room resources. I've found great meeting spaces in unlikely places. For example, a major sports arena rents out meeting spaces with a view of the stadium, and the rental cost is minimal, not including the catering. As part of its mission, a private foundation allows nonprofits to reserve space at no cost, as long as the reservation is made in advance. The foundation hosts water, coffee, and tea service throughout the day as part of its nonprofit support.

If your organization has a limited budget, you can find creative venue solutions. Leverage the organization's board members, community partners, clients, donors, and suppliers.

Many large institutions, such as universities, major museums, hospitals, banks, and architectural firms, as well as firms with large co-working spaces, may provide a meeting facility at no cost, with the hope of cultivating a relationship with your organization and its leaders. One of my clients found a great workshop space at their city's Better Business Bureau headquarters. The bureau's staff welcomed the group and an executive provided introductory remarks—a win-win for all parties.

One of my biotech clients needed a small, innovative space for their offsite strategic planning meeting. A nearby medical school provided the space for a minimal rental fee, including full technology support and plenty of whiteboarding space. The day included a guided behind-the-scenes tour of the medical school's teaching facility during a break. This created an exceptional experience for my client, at a very low cost.

You'll also want to ensure that your space has ample room to move around and additional space for breakout discussions or separate group sessions. Make sure that your space has plenty of lighting to create a bright and innovative atmosphere, and that meeting rooms feature the appropriate technology for on-screen presentations and audio (microphone) needs. Once you've determined the location for your workshop, reserve the venue. Always preview the facility a few days prior to your workshop so that you are familiar with the available space and the room dynamics.

Meeting Room Dynamics

- Create your main, full-group room configuration (such as a round table seating chart, U-shape layout, or boardroom style) that encourages participants to easily communicate and get to know each other.

- Plan adequate time to meticulously set up the room. Effective room and facility setup is integral for an interactive plenary session and other sessions, and this should be completed well before the workshop begins. Don't miscalculate the time it will take to prepare and position audio-visual equipment, flip charts, on-screen projectors, speaker requirements, supplies, and snacks. It's not uncommon for setup to take three hours or more, depending on the size of your group and activities planned. One way to create a bit of intrigue is by covering your flip charts prior to the start of the meeting. Only reveal them when you're ready to share the content. This eliminates distraction and also adds anticipation and surprise to your meeting dynamics.

- Set up breakout areas, and ensure that you make efficient use of your allocated space. For breakout groups, make sure each group has plenty of space to move around the room and to add to flip charts. Avoid putting breakout areas too close together or too far apart, as you'll want to be able to rotate groups quickly while preserving space for focus and privacy for small-group conversations.

- Create name tags for your participants and table tent cards with each participant's name. Even if all attendees know one another, the name tags and tent cards help guest participants and speakers with easy reference. I've found that name tag and table tent card printing is an activity best suited for those who are providing administrative support for the strategic planning workshop, so that you, the strategist, can focus your time on creating workshop content and planning how to maximize the use of your meeting facility. You should expect to have name tags and table tent cards in hand a few days prior to your event. Prior to the start of your workshop, place these appropriately to determine your desired seating arrangements and facilitate good conversation. Name tags can be distributed at a check-in table staffed by your organization's administrative support team, or whomever you appoint to assist with meet-and-greet activities.

- Provide a brief meet-and-greet arrival window of around 15 to 30 minutes. I encourage you not to leave this part out of your workshop schedule. It allows your participants to arrive, grab refreshments, chat, and have time before settling into their designated table spot.

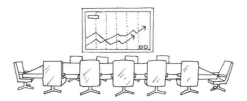

YOUR WORKSHOP NEEDS QUALITY CONTENT

Use my Vital Strategic Plan workshop framework as a starting point and develop a detailed agenda. You will want to describe every activity, and each agenda item should build upon the prior activity. Review the detailed agenda with your top executive or steering committee, incorporating their input and ensuring that each piece of the program has their full support. Decide whether there should be external guest participation.

With a proliferation of videos, podcasts, and presentations available online—all competing for our attention—the bar has been raised regarding what constitutes a quality speaker. All invited guest speakers and panelists should serve as credible sources of insight applicable to your organization. As your organization's curator, you have every reason to choose wisely, for the sake of a powerfully credible kickoff! All speakers should be experts at crisply bringing to life external issues facing your industry.

I highly recommend external guest speakers to help your executive team kick off the workshop by sharing external market insight. And I can't say this enough: do *not* start your strategic planning workshop with a discussion of vision. If you must discuss vision, do this toward the end of your workshop.

Develop a Meaningful Pre-Workshop Homework Assignment and Share It with the Participants

I've found that pre-workshop team assignments for completing important analysis can be one of the most efficient and effective ways to spread out the workload. While dividing up the analysis work, executive team assignments create participant skin in the game and buy-in, shared learning, and team bonding. A pre-workshop homework assignment can create a much higher level of internal support and anticipation for your strategic planning workshop, because each participant is required to bring something of value to the table.

During the workshop, when team members share their homework insights, I've witnessed magical moments of shared "ah-has" when a room full of people come to a new realization, such as discovering an emerging issue or future threat. These shared moments based on competitive data, a survey response, or a best practice can set the tone for the remainder of the strategic planning workshop.

External insight enables leaders to shift from what they already know based on past thinking, to seek new external knowledge and act on novel, fresh external perspectives.[3] This helps leaders and their organizations lead and grow into the future.

In summary, executive homework creates a richer workshop experience by spreading the investigative workload when leaders analyze strategic issues, threats, and opportunities. Executive homework helps to foster quality discussions, shared learning, critical thinking, and management buy-in—as well as accountability, a bit of peer pressure, and personal commitment.

- Work with your strategic plan steering committee to develop a useful homework assignment for your executive team.

- Divide strategic planning workshop participants into teams of four to five members. Select team members to work on assigned topics where people can get to know each other, where professional skills and experience are maximized.

- Make assignments at least a month prior to your strategic planning workshop. Allow ample time for team members to work together to complete the assignment. A number of executive homework assignments, including scenario-planning, gap analysis, and competitive intelligence, are noted in the appendix.

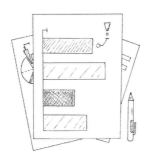

Consider Pre-Meeting Survey Research Needed for Input

This includes things such as customer or constituent surveys, employee surveys, and focus groups. Summarize results and present the findings during your workshop. A homework team could analyze data and be accountable for presenting the findings.

Financial data prepared in advance can play a critical role in assessing strategic opportunities. Comprehensive financial analysis will require time outside of your strategic planning workshop, whether conducted on a pre-workshop or post-workshop basis.

For example, financial analysis could include free cash flow, economic value added, asset management, financing decisions and capital structure, profitability ratios, growth indices (market share growth), risk assessment and management, and tax optimization.[4] If the financial data is too detailed for your strategic planning workshop, it could be shared at a follow-up meeting as a drill-down session following the strategic planning workshop.

A Vital, Flexible Strategic Planning Workshop Framework

To be clear, there's no such thing as a one-size-fits-all strategic planning workshop template. However, a vital strategic planning workshop features four necessary workshop process steps, and this creates a helpful framework:

First, a thorough assessment of the external environment pertinent to your organization.

Second, a realistic view of the current status of your organization in the context of your environment.

Third, determining your company's desired vision and future in the next three years.

Fourth, developing strategic goals to move your organization forward to the desired destination.

After you meet with your executive team, you'll be armed with insight. You'll be equipped to custom craft an exciting workshop to meet the needs of your organization's culture, time availability, budget, and organizational dynamics.

I believe it's important to plan for a bit of agenda flexibility. This will require you to think in advance about your workshop logistics. Ask yourself: How might I respond with agility, and what might I adjust if time is running short, or if an agenda item is not working for the group?

Most strategic planning workshops can be accomplished in less than two days. For example, a typical one-day workshop would begin at 8 a.m. and continue until the late afternoon, including lunch and several breaks.

Pre-workshop homework could be shared with your executive team a month prior to your workshop. That way, participants will arrive to the workshop ready to share homework insights.

A typical two-day workshop could begin at lunch, or midafternoon on the first day (for example, 2 p.m. on Friday). The workshop would end at 4 p.m. or earlier on the second day (for example, 4 p.m. on Saturday).

Large organizations may prefer to develop a series of strategy meetings spread out over several months. When sequenced as a series, topics such as trends, scenario-planning, and discovery activities can be staged in two- to three-hour time blocks to allow for shared learning and deep-dive discussions.

As you review my time-saving framework on the following pages, you can use these ideas to customize a vibrant workshop perfectly suited for your organization. You can use a variety of strategic planning tools, techniques, and activities provided in this book as well as in the appendix. Embellish these, and make them your own.

After your executive team or client has approved the workshop agenda, print a basic, high-level agenda for your attendees. This can be placed at each table setting during the workshop, or inserted into your strategic planning notebook or folder for each attendee.

While your participants will receive a basic agenda, you and your workshop facilitation team and meeting scribe should use a very detailed agenda with every activity spelled out and a time frame for each agenda item. Your detailed agenda should include names, titles, and phone numbers of all guest speakers, in case you need to call a speaker who hasn't arrived yet. You can also include reminder notes and needed announcements—such as where the restrooms are located—for facilitating each part of the agenda.

Whether you develop a one-day strategic planning summit, a two-day workshop, or a series of meetings, this framework will help you, the curator, expedite and tailor a vital strategic planning leadership experience.

Always keep in mind that the genius of this process is *you*—not any given tool or template! And the genius of the strategy making is your organization's strategic planning team.

Vital Strategic Planning Workshop Overview

1. Welcome and introductions (including an executive endorsement)

2. External trends presentation (guest panel or keynote speaker)

3. Brainstorm and Bucket Exercise

4. External analysis and research findings—presentations by homework teams

     For example, presentations could include these or other specific analysis reports:

   - Focus group and listening session results

   - SWOT Analysis

   - PESTEL Analysis

   - Competitive Intelligence to compare similar or competing organizations

5. Strategy development: pillar breakout groups, leading to prioritized strategic goals

6. Optional discussion: hot topics

7. Optional discussion: vision, mission, values, grand purpose ("Vision, Etc.")

8. Discuss ongoing goal-tracking and communication

9. Wrap-up:

- Discuss next steps and approval of the written strategic plan

- Thank participants and adjourn

(This agenda overview does not include breaks, lunch, evening reception, or other activities.)

Following is a detailed guide for you, the workshop curator, so that you can fully develop each workshop agenda activity. I encourage you to modify this framework to accomplish your strategic planning workshop goals.

DETAILED STRATEGIC PLANNING AGENDA

This detailed agenda framework is only *for you*, the facilitator or curator, for your planning purposes. Do not share this step-by-step description of activities with your participants.

Welcome and Introductions

(Estimated time: 15 minutes depending on group size.)

Maximize the impact of your opening act. Take cues from big sporting events, concerts, and galas where the organizers are creating sizzle, sparkle, and splash from the moment attendees arrive.

- Create hospitality from the get-go. Appoint a few greeters to welcome all participants as they arrive. This makes everyone feel valued and important. Your participants won't be expecting a grand entrance where they are welcomed with celebrity status and thanked in advance for their participation.

- Give everyone a welcome gift, even if your budget is small. This could be a T-shirt with your company's logo, or a small bag filled with healthy snacks—anything that creates fun and hospitality. Your attendees will be pleasantly surprised to receive a "hello" gift. From the moment they arrive, they'll realize that your strategic planning workshop is not just another interruption to their day.

As your meeting begins, here are a few tips to create gravitas for the important work to be accomplished. I've seen far too many strategic planning meetings begin abruptly, without the appropriate decorum and unity among the participants.

- Create an attractive place setting for all participants, including an agenda and meeting folder with materials, as well as tent cards featuring each person's name.

- Invite your organization's CEO, board chairman, or top executive to share a brief, inspirational welcome. Plan this in advance. Have your top executive state the workshop goals. This demonstrates executive endorsement and leadership by example. A warm welcome also creates an inclusive, no-silo environment where participants feel valued from the start. Have your executive thank participants for their investment of time.

- Invite participants to introduce themselves, and during this time create a large-group opening experience so that all in the room experience human connectivity, appreciation, and respect. Keep this experience simple and fun. The appendix features a number of opening activities.

- Avoid calling your opening act an "icebreaker," which assumes your attendees have a frozen attitude. Icebreakers can be perceived as forced, boring games or exercises rather than an authentic experience to unify participating leaders.

- Introduce the facilitator. The facilitator should greet the group, set a positive tone, and introduce key elements about the agenda and meeting logistics, such as restroom locations and scheduled breaks.

- Ask the group to establish a few ground rules for the planning session, such as no texting or phone calls during workshop sessions. The appendix provides additional ground rule ideas.

External Trends Presentation

(Estimated time: 90 minutes. This includes a 60-minute presentation with 30-minute Q&A session.)

Following the welcome and participant introductions, invite your external trends speaker or panel of experts to take the stage. This presentation should be planned well in advance of the workshop.

Ideal speakers could include trade association executives, business and nonprofit collaborators, supply chain partners, elected officials, and notable leaders related to your field. The guest speaker or panel will share a compelling, fast-paced overview of external industry trends, market intelligence, competitive insights, and external pressures impacting your industry.

External speakers help to open up thinking, as well as provide thinking space after introductions. This provides an opportunity for participants to settle in, learn together, and consider big-impact trends and issues impacting your industry. Following this opening presentation, invite and facilitate audience questions and dialogue.

Break

(Estimated time: 10 to 15 minutes.)

Following your opening presentation, take a brief break. This is a great opportunity for your external panelists to exit, stage right! Or, if your workshop could benefit from their participation in the next exercise, invite your speakers to stay for the next brainstorm exercise.

Whether your speakers stay or leave, do plan this in advance so that speakers can be properly thanked and can leave the meeting at a defined point. During the break, participants can mingle with speakers, reflect on the discussion, grab snacks, stretch their legs, access restroom facilities, and check phone messages. However, everyone should be back in the room at the designated time.

Brainstorm and Bucket Exercise

(Estimated time: 30 minutes.)

The facilitator begins this exercise by asking participants to consider the organization's future horizon by asking this question: What must we, as an organization, do to succeed—achieve our vision and thrive? Call on raised hands and ask individuals to shout out their visionary ideas. Assign two or three staff members or workshop participants to serve as scribes who will capture each idea on giant Post-it notes.

Spoiler alert! This activity will lead to your team developing strategic goals in support of your organization's four pillars: Programs, Products, and Services; Financial; Operational Effectiveness; and External Outreach (Communication, Marketing, and Branding). Following this exercise, you can add the pillars into your Leadership Map template and share with your workshop participants.

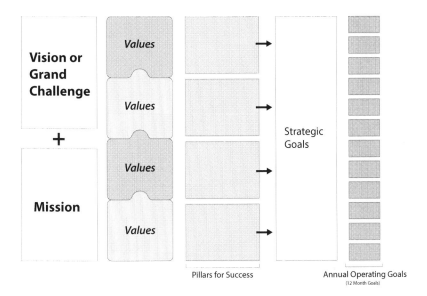

Leadership Map © Carol A. Poore.

This exercise allows participants to focus on the visionary future in a perfect world—as if there were no risks of failing. Set the ground rule that there are *no* wrong answers in considering this visionary horizon.

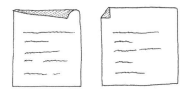

The facilitator will continue to repeat the question: What *must* we do to *succeed,* achieving our vision in the future? Let the exercise continue for 15 minutes or so, until no further ideas are shouted out. Be patient during pauses. Give people a chance to think deeply. Do not be intimidated by a bit of silence. The volunteers will still be helping you write the individual ideas on Post-it notes. To dig further, you can interject a related question: What things *must* we get right during the next three years?

Remember, this is a brainstorm. Collect all ideas without discussing or judging the merits of them. All answers should be captured and documented quickly by staff, and then be sorted on blank flip charts posted on the wall. When ideas are exhausted, your scribes will give everyone a few Post-it notes featuring the brainstormed key words and phrases. Ask the group to sort the Post-it notes by theme, using four blank flip-chart pages posted on a nearby wall.

Remember that this is not a problem-solving discussion. This is a major pillar-creating exercise. With your expert facilitation, this entire exercise should be able to be completed in 30 minutes. Participants will post, repost, and make adjustments until participants are mostly satisfied that the Post-its are organized into major themes. Leave a few inches of bare space at the top of each flip chart by drawing a line four inches or so from the top. Ask participants to put the Post-it notes below your line. As the ideas are sorted and named, the organization's four major strategic themes or pillars will emerge. Ask the group to name the theme. Write the theme name or title at the top of each chart. Observe the themes as a group.

Your flip-chart titles or major themes will look very similar to, if not identical to, these four pillars:

1. Programs, Products, and Services

2. Financial

3. Operational Effectiveness

4. External Outreach (Communication, Marketing, and Branding).

These are major drivers of all organizations, no matter the type. These four themes will become the pillars for the organization's strategic goals. By now, your group should be charged up and looking forward to the rest of the workshop.

In my three decades of strategic planning work with a variety of clients, I've found that all companies feature these four pillars, although it might not have been widely recognized among the leaders prior to this exercise. These pillars offer the opportunity for boundary spanning across the organization, where leader accountability for strategic goals may traverse departments and divisions.

For example, the Financial pillar is not driven solely by the finance department. That's because the business functions of a finance department typically include planning, organizing, auditing, accounting for, and controlling its company's finances and producing financial statements. However, the revenue-generating functions include your organization's client-facing divisions such as the program, product, and services; marketing; and sales departments. Together, all of these functions will feature goals contributing to the Financial pillar—your organization's financial health.

These four pillars are simple to understand and are exceptionally comprehensive. The Vital Strategic Plan pillars share similar attributes to Kaplan and Norton's Balanced Scorecard model. Both models provide effective major systems from which to structure strategic and operational goals. While sharing similarities, the Vital Strategic Plan pillar model features two distinct differences.

First, the Vital Strategic Plan pillar model consolidates all operational effectiveness functions into one strategic pillar. Second, the Vital Strategic Plan pillar model shines a spotlight on External

Outreach, which includes communication, marketing, and brand-ing. External Outreach is a critical part of an organization's success. External Outreach is not called out in the Balanced Scorecard.

THE VITAL STRATEGIC PLAN PILLARS	
Programs, Products, and Services	A revenue-generating product, program, or service put on the market for acquisition, attention, or consumption. These meet a market or customer need or want, whether offered by a for-profit company, nonprofit organization, or government agency.
Financial	The current and projected financial status, and future growth opportunities. All strategies supporting revenue generation and financial health of the organization are included here.
Operational Effectiveness	Internal processes, such as customer service, billing, product delivery, and supply chain. Human Resources (including employee development and learn-ing functions such as LEAN Six Sigma, and Agile training and ethos.).
External Outreach	Branding, community and public relations, advertising, market-ing, and all strategic communications (both internal and exter-nal) on all platforms.

BALANCED SCORECARD PERSPECTIVES	
Customer and Stakeholder	Customer value, satisfaction and/or retention; performance from the perspective of the customer or key stakeholders the organiza-tion is designed to serve.
Financial or stewardship	Financial performance and effective resource use.
Internal process	Efficiency and quality related to the product, services, or other key business processes.
Organizational capacity or learning and growth	Human capital, infrastructure, technology, culture and other capacities key to breakthrough performance.

If you are conducting a two-day workshop,
adjourn the meeting now.

Consider hosting an evening reception or dinner for all partici-pants. This can provide a relaxing opportunity to mix, mingle, and network—especially helpful for those who traveled to attend the meeting in a host city. For a two-day workshop, open the program on Day 2 by asking participants to share their top new insights from Day 1. This discussion should be fast-paced and not exceed 10 minutes. This technique allows participants to warm up and affirm the most valuable insights from Day 1.

If you are conducting a one-day workshop,
continue to the next agenda item.

External Analysis Research Findings (Homework Teams)

(Estimated time: 90 minutes. Each assigned homework team will present a 10-minute presentation with five minutes for Q&A and discussion.)

Invite your homework teams to share the assigned external analysis presentations. This part of your program should create team bonding as participants begin to discuss competitive forces that present anxiety, threat, struggle, and challenge, as well as creating shared hope and opportunities for future success.

Chapter 2 provided a variety of strategic planning homework activities, such as competitive intelligence, external focus groups, and SWOT and PESTEL analysis.

Break

(Estimated time: 15 minutes.)

Strategy Development: Pillar Breakout Groups

(Estimated time: approximately 90 minutes to 2 hours.)

This pillar breakout activity represents the pinnacle of your entire strategic planning workshop and should lead to prioritized strategic goals. Your participants will develop strategies for each of the four pillar areas using a thought-provoking method that gets the ball rolling very efficiently and effectively while allowing ample time to think deeply and apply insights from the prior trends and analysis sessions.

Strategy is not formed overnight. The art of shaping strategic goals—your organization's strategic intent—requires your team to make assumptions about the future, including financial and market projections.

However, changes in our world do happen overnight. This can render one or more strategic goals obsolete. Once your strategic goals are shaped, you'll review them at strategic intervals, because your goals are not static or airtight against change. Flexibility also will be key for quickly adapting strategic goals to twists, turns, and tweaks that might be needed.

Strategy formation always is performed in a dynamic environment, as Henry Mintzberg noted decades ago. While organizations strive for stability in a system of bureaucracy, the role of leadership is to maintain a strong and stable organization while operating in constant change.[5]

Your organization's work in defining its strategy, as well as the opportunity to learn as a team, may be the most important action you take all year. In just two hours, your team will create flexible strategic goals that allow for adaptation when assumptions are no longer valid.

This next exercise is designed to make the best use of the valuable time you have together, even if this is only one full day where undivided attention is focused on doing the bulk of the work.

I developed the Fail-Succeed strategy discussion as a succinct, energizing approach to helping your team create powerful strategies that get translated into strategic goals. I've adapted the technique to fit numerous types, structures, and sizes of organizations, with outstanding results.

It's important to note that some organizations may use a specific and highly institutionalized process for strategy and goal-shaping.

If this is the case for your organization, you can either customize the Fail-Succeed discussion to fit into your organization's systemized process, or you can replace Fail-Succeed with your company's existing strategy approach. No matter what your goal-shaping methodology may be, *do* ensure that your goals align with and support your organization's four pillars.

Fail-Succeed Strategy Discussion

> *Part I—Fail:* Participants take all rose-colored glasses off to look at the worst-case scenario for each of your organization's four pillars.

> Potential failure points are specifically captured on the flip charts.

> *Part II—Succeed:* Participants become very creative, striving to overcome doomsday for each pillar.

> Success strategies will be turned into SMART, prioritized goals.

Four groups will be preassigned by your organization's executive team or top leader, with your guidance. I recommend that you preassign the senior leaders and board members to the breakout room where their knowledge is well matched to the pillar.

Separate into four pillar breakout groups (Programs, Products, and Services; Financial; Operational Effectiveness; and External Outreach). Group composition should be planned ahead of time based on the four pillar themes discussed earlier, and professional perspectives needed to thoroughly discuss each pillar.

For example, the Programs, Products, and Services pillar break-out group should include management responsible for developing these aspects of your organization, along with staff members and guests who may share this development and sales expertise.

The Financial pillar breakout group should have at least one or more participating executives with a background of oversee-ing financial operations. This could include the organization's chief financial officer, board treasurer, and external guests with financial backgrounds.

The External Outreach pillar breakout group should include at least one or more leaders with PR, marketing, branding, and com-munity relations expertise. The Operational Effectiveness pillar breakout group should include one or more leaders with matching areas of expertise.

While it can be helpful to mix a variety of skills in each of the pillar groups, the exercise will be incomplete if specific skill sets cor-responding to each of the four pillars are completely missing. Be strategic about *who* participates in each breakout group, and assign someone to be a discussion facilitator for each group.

Participants are now ready to complete a Fail-Succeed strat-egy exercise focused on each of the four pillars. My Fail-Succeed activity is especially effective for small to midsized organizations, because it quickly takes the blinders off to reveal the "fail" factors that can hinder an organization's ability to produce outcomes. The "succeed" portion of the exercise creates specific solutions or strat-egies for success, which then can be prioritized and shaped into SMART (Specific, Measurable, Attainable, Results-oriented, and Time-Based) strategic goals for each pillar.

In the Fail discussion, breakout groups will discuss each of the four pillars in detail using a "doomsday versus success" discussion format. For each pillar being discussed, the breakout group facili-tator will begin by asking the group: For *this* pillar, how will our

organization *fail?* Participants are asked to share specific answers—
not generalities. One family-owned sandwich shop cited very
specific failure points, such as "expanding our stores too rapidly
where cash flow is depleted."

The discussion leader for each pillar breakout group will continue to probe the "how might we fail" question until each group
has exhausted all possible answers.

I've been asked why anyone would want to start with a negative
lens rather than focus on positives, such as the "happy story" exercise where everyone dreams up a visionary tale. I argue that the Fail
part of this exercise will expose your organization's urgent, strategic,
and potentially catastrophic priorities first, so that your team will be
laser-focused on the right success strategies for each of your organization's four pillars.

There will be plenty of time to discuss your organization's vibrant
future, moving well beyond the failure points to develop forward-
thinking success strategies and strategic opportunities that advance
your firm's competitive future. Those success strategies may include
what strategy professors Chan Kim and Renée Mauborgne define as
"blue ocean strategies," to potentially open up a completely new
market space and create uncontested new demand, making the
competition irrelevant.[6]

After failure points are articulated and documented, each breakout team will develop a very specific strategic success strategy to
counteract and overcome each individual potential failure. Success
strategies are brought to life with my next steps: Round-Robin and
Voting.

Round-Robin

(Estimated time: 20 to 25 minutes.)

Round-Robin is a fast-paced group rotation technique for
quickly vetting breakout group content. It's also a fun and easy way

to generate lots of strategies, ideas, and input while giving all participants a voice for important topics to be discussed. I always pair this activity with the Fail-Succeed exercise.

When you're ready for small-group discussion such as the Fail-Succeed discussion, assign teams to designated breakout areas where flip charts are set up and ready with markers. Each group will be assigned a strategic pillar. For each pillar, both "fail" and "success" questions will be answered during the Round-Robin session.

As mentioned earlier, the first part of the exercise will focus on what it would take to fail regarding the pillar at hand. For the Financial pillar, for example, the breakout room facilitator will ask and continue to ask: What would it take for our organization to fail in financial strength—or in the future financial vision for our company?

Give the group plenty of time to discuss the subject and make recommendations on flip charts. Be sure to provide ample instructions and structure so that each breakout group will be able to deliver the desired input.

Next, close out the breakout discussion. Ask each group to rotate clockwise (or "rotate to the right") into the next breakout group for five minutes or so. Each group will have an opportunity to review work completed by the prior group. Ask participants to comment on the other pillars, and add any failure ideas or input that may be missing before rotating back to the home-base room.

Allow five minutes for each rotating group to add comments and insight to the existing flip chart. Then, keep the groups rotating clockwise (hence, "Round-Robin") to the next room in five-minute increments until each group returns to the home-base room. This activity adds peer review and multiplies comments for each breakout topic while also allowing each group to have input on all breakout topics. It's fun, fast-paced, and keeps everyone actively moving. You, the facilitator, will direct the groups when it's time to continue rotating.

Next, for each failure point, the pillar team will create a very specific success strategy. Note that the success strategy should not simply state the opposite of each failure point. Each success strategy should be SMART, and should specifically counter the failure point.

For example, if the failure point is "revenue declines because XYZ product or service becomes obsolete," the strategic success strategy might be "assess XYZ product or service for market resiliency and create a substitute revenue source to replace and expand revenue by X percent." When there are no more success ideas being vetted, each of the breakout groups will rotate, in a second Round-Robin activity, to view and provide input at all other pillar breakout rooms, contributing additional success points on the flip charts if key ideas are missing.

Groups can spend five minutes in each room before returning to their original home-base room. Each major breakout topic will feature a deep-dive discussion by the first group, followed by brief peer reviews by the other teams as they complete the five-minute rotations. This is a highly participative, democratic activity allowing all voices to be heard.

Vote to Prioritize Each Pillar's Success Strategies

(Estimated time: 15 minutes.)

This voting exercise is designed to provide a clear sense of the most urgent strategic priorities and opportunities. The purpose of voting with sticky dots is *not* to build consensus or foster groupthink.

Give participants a reasonable number of small, colored sticky dots (around twenty), and ask them to prioritize or support top strategic plan initiatives that have been written on flip charts. Each person will vote by tacking a dot next to an idea or strategic goal. Limit each person to no more than three dots posted on any given item to avoid having anyone "game the system" by placing all of their dots on their favorite goal.

At the end of the voting exercise, participants will see which success strategies appear to be the most important according to the votes. Encourage the group to vote independently. Strategic plan three-year goals will be prioritized by the number of individual sticky dots placed on the list of success strategies.

Discuss Goal Priorities in a Plenary Group

(Estimated time: 15 minutes.)

What happens next, after the vote? Now is the time to gather as a plenary group to briefly share the top vote getters. While this voting exercise is not scientific, it quickly shows your leadership team's goal priorities. Gaining a clear sense of goal priority is the pivotal point during any strategic planning process. This is especially true for organizations supported by volunteer board members, all with various opinions, good ideas, personal agendas, and limited time for providing ongoing support.

Prioritized goals are powerful statements of strategic intent. They provide a clear focus to achieve what's important: strategic impact.

Once the success priorities have been identified and prioritized by participants, there's no need to spend further time wordsmithing during the workshop. The hard work of identifying the strategic goals to support each of your organization's pillars has been accomplished. Now, all participants have firsthand knowledge about each pillar's priority goals.

These strategic goals—in raw form—will be further refined by executive management or the appointed staff in days to come, *outside* of the strategic planning workshop. Each success strategy considered to be top priority will be priority ranked and carefully crafted or fine-tuned into a three-year SMART goal.

For each strategic goal, your staff must assess what can and should be accomplished in the next twelve months. Your organization's staff can then shape twelve-month annual operating goals to support each three-year strategic goal.

For each pillar, these one-year goals will become your organization's twelve-month operational plan. The annual plan should be tracked at least quarterly. Annual goals will be updated in years two and three, with focus on accomplishing each strategic goal at the end of year three.

For example, a nonprofit organization may want to raise $6 million in three years. The fundraising goal for year one might be $2 million (one-third of the total). If the organization raises the entire $6 million in the first year, the executive team can celebrate success. Then, the team may choose to elevate the strategic fundraising goal to a higher level, increasing the goal for years two and three.

Break Options

(Estimated time: 15 minutes for a break; 60 minutes if lunch is served.)

Arrange a lunch presentation—either a speaker or panel to address a strategic issue or current hot topics leading to afternoon discussions—or, for a one-day workshop, take a break.

Address Hot Topics or Proceed to Final Agenda Items

(Estimated time: 60 minutes.)

Organizations often face critical issues of an urgent nature, such as immediate cash flow issues, staffing challenges, and communication breakdowns. The CEO may want to discuss short-term planning topics such as reviewing a sales or donor pipeline, or get into the nuts and bolts of product, program, and service planning. These are hot topics—significant and perhaps dire—but are not strategic issues.

I highly recommend that you don't waste your prime strategic discussion time focused on solving tactical issues. While hot topics usually include urgent tactical issues, these can drain the life out of strategic thinking. Instead, carve out an hour toward the end of your workshop, and reserve this tight hour for a fast-paced hot-topic discussion. Do this after your strategic goal-shaping and prioritization activities, to keep your group's strategic thinking on track.

Assign hot-topic breakout groups prior to your workshop, if possible. Select participants with deep subject knowledge and assign them to support a relevant hot-topic group.

When I led a statewide chamber of commerce strategic planning retreat, our afternoon hot topics focused on the chamber's regulatory agenda. Board and staff members were assigned to hot-topic rooms where their professional backgrounds and lobbying and lawmaking expertise were able to shape specific messages and outreach strategies for the upcoming legislative session.

Consider inviting *external hot-topic guests* to join this part of the meeting to add specific insight and fresh ideas for an hour or so. Your external experts can add a much-needed spark of creativity in solving problems of an urgent nature.

Final Brainstorm for Vision, Etc.

(Estimated time: 15–20 minutes.)

If your executive team or steering committee needs to discuss your organization's vision, mission, or grand purpose (I call this Vision, Etc.), now is the time to conduct a group brainstorm. It's important to note (once again) that most organizations embarking on a strategic planning process *do not* need their vision overhauled. Therefore, if your organization needs to redefine or sharpen its vision statement, I highly recommend that vision discussions be conducted as a *closing activity*, and as a brainstorm activity.

While energy in the room may be waning, the group is now in a strategic mindset. Trust has been cultivated and the table has been set for great ideas to now emerge. Plus, the group will be eager to wrap up the day! Keep the brainstorming fast-paced. Brainstorming provides a low-risk way to canvass ideas without judgmental feedback or arguments.

This takes the pressure off of having to wordsmith the perfect verbiage. Staff can summarize results and later refine the concepts info several draft versions for further discussion.

Vision, Etc. represents all discussions that could take place regarding your organization's overarching vision, mission, values, grand challenges, and BHAGs (big, hairy, audacious goals), which are separate and much different than strategic goals.

- Vision: Where the organization wants to be in the future—the horizon.

- Mission: What the organization *does* or delivers; its purpose.

- Grand Challenge: An inspirational be-all, end-all grand purpose statement or ultimate reason for being. (Not all organizations feature a Grand Challenge; this trend has evolved since the turn of this century, building upon the fields of science and technology.)

- Values: Behaviors, standards, beliefs, and codes of conduct declared as vital and important for the organization to thrive and succeed, of which all employees are expected to embody.

- BHAGs: Aspirational goals that constitute gigantic wins.

General Vision, Etc. Brainstorm Activity

Prearrange Post-it flip charts around the room with headings as noted in the following table. You, the facilitator, are only interested in gathering rapid-fire input. Ask participants to shout out key words and brief phrases. Be ready to quickly capture all input. Because this exercise is fast-paced, consider assigning two scribes to tag-team in capturing the input on the flip charts. Move quickly around the room between flip charts until you've exhausted all ideas being

shouted from the floor. You can circle back a second time to continue the momentum.

FLIP-CHART HEADINGS	QUESTIONS TO ASK FOR EACH HEADING
Vision	What vision will allow us to serve existing, new, and growing needs for customers, clients, and markets?
Mission	What do we *do* that is exceptional to change lives and meet needs?
Grand Challenge	What is our organization's highest purpose or reason for being? Why do we exist? What will our organization's lasting legacy be that sets us apart from every other organization?
Values	What values are most important to our clients, constituents, suppliers, employees, and everyone we serve? What are our most important values as an organization?
BHAGs	What *huge* accomplishment or goal should we pursue?

A Values-Only Brainstorm

This exercise works well for organizations where the vision and mission
don't need updating, but values do. It allows for speedy input with
no time for arguments or lengthy discussion. Have participants use a
marker and write their top five values as they see them for the organization. This exercise should be completed within 10 to 15 minutes.

After the group is finished, provide each person with ten sticky
dots for individual voting, and ask each person to vote on the top
values, placing no more than two dots on any one value. This exercise allows quiet individual reflection while providing the opportunity
for collective recap of the priority votes. Following the meeting, staff
can summarize the values and add these into the strategic plan written draft for final review and discussion.

If a Vision, Etc. conversation is not needed as a closing activity,
ask the group to share what the organization might *stop* doing in
order to focus strategic priorities. This critical conversation is often

overlooked as executive teams look toward the future. Capture ideas on flip charts for further deliberation by staff following the strategic planning meeting.

Wrapping Up the Day

(Estimated time: 10 minutes.)

When it's time to wrap up the workshop, your organization's chief executive officer or top executive should discuss next steps for goal-tracking, communication, and celebrating results, such as:

- Affirm how all discussion notes will be drafted into a written plan, including who will be accountable for writing the first draft, the process for review and approval, and deadlines for the first draft and final plan. For example, while some organizations ask the strategic planning steering committee to review, edit, and approve the final plan, other firms may provide an opportunity for participants to share feedback through an internal, web-based input system.

- Discuss plans for instituting an ongoing tracking system. Share how goals will be institutionalized—that is, monitored, tracked, and reported using measurement tools such as dashboards. Discuss the organization's frequency of review including division, department, and work-group levels.

- Thank everyone for participating.

Adjourn the Meeting on a High Note

Close out the meeting on a high note, thanking everyone for their contributions. If the budget permits, provide a meaningful farewell gift for the participants.

HOW TO DEAL WITH NONSTRATEGIC HOT TOPICS

As you end the workshop, you may face a common dilemma: how to incorporate the CEO's request for a nitty-gritty, problem-solving conversation to address any number of dire issues. These are also hot topics. These are large, looming, and tactical issues that are oh-so-important, but can bog down your strategic planning workshop. I'm talking about things like cash flow, hiring issues, fundraising problems, or any late-breaking crisis impacting the organization. Other examples of nonstrategic hot topics could include:

- The latest negative news announcement about your firm.

- A late-breaking competitive threat.

- Urgent short-term fundraising needs, especially for nonprofits.

- The plan for how to best scale up an organization to become regional, national, or international.

- Recruiting new members and retaining existing members with special focus on young professionals.

- Key messaging for an organization.

- How to grow a new program.

- Revenue-generating services that add value to membership.

- Membership engagement in an era of diverse membership needs and competition from many information sources.

- Expanding communication strategies to include digital outreach techniques and use of influencers to help share strategic plan key messages.

I witnessed this with a nonprofit organization that was facing a deep financial cash flow crisis when it held a board strategic planning retreat. This healthcare organization had only a few months of operating capital in the bank. The CEO felt pressure to increase board member support, thinking it could resolve the financial emergency. But rather than discussing the cash crisis at the beginning of the strategic planning board agenda, when panic and negativity could have derailed the entire workshop, the conversation was scheduled as the closing activity on the first day.

This approach proved to be productive. The CEO presented a candid overview of current finances followed by a board brainstorm. This resulted in dozens of fundraising ideas and board commitment for individual board members to make future asks.

Do not allow short-term emergency issues to sidetrack your strategic planning workshop! Instead, create a space near the end of your strategic planning workshop for conducting a hot topic discussion. This technique protects your strategic discussions from straying off course.

- Schedule your hot-topic discussion to occur *after* significant strategic goal work is completed, such as during the late afternoon on the second day of your workshop.

- Break the group into smaller problem-solving teams. Allow no more than an hour for the hot-topic discussion.

- If hot topics are controversial, ask breakout groups to *brainstorm potential solutions* rather than directly solve problems. Keep the discussion positive, fast-paced, and idea oriented.

- Remind participants that either-or thinking is not productive. However, *integrative thinking*, or the process of combining ideas from a number of people, can generate multiple possibilities.[7]

- Consider inviting external hot-topic experts to jump into your meeting for an hour or so. This is a wonderful opportunity to customize the workshop by inviting a group of thought leaders who can provide insight about critically important issues, risks, and opportunities specific to your organization. These could be leaders of your organization's supply chain, or trade association executives pertinent to your business. Topic experts could be elected officials, public administrators, or university scholars. Put together a dream team of experts with diverse perspectives, and invite them to join a prestigious think tank. This is an effective way to introduce topic experts to your organization, while they provide an intense focus on problem solving.

• Bring groups back into a plenary session and ask each small group to share the top three ideas generated. Notes can be summarized and acted upon by staff. Then, move on to the next part of your strategic planning session.

HOT-TOPIC SESSION EXPANDS A SMALL NONPROFIT'S INFLUENCE

I was hired to develop a strategic planning program for a nonprofit organization that helps formerly incarcerated women thrive with job and life skills after they leave the justice system. I worked closely with the CEO to identify leaders who could address three hot-topic issues, including the opportunity to create workforce opportunities, public awareness, and public policy and advocacy.

We invited several private foundation and corporate leaders and state legislators whose passion is criminal justice reform to join our fast-paced hot-topic session. A facilitator for each topic group was appointed to lead a breakout discussion with questions planned in advance for participating guests, board, and staff.

Following the hot-topic breakout discussions, the entire group joined together for 30 minutes in a final plenary session where each group shared three action steps recommended for the organization. The hot-topic exercise generated dozens of new ideas for the organization, and provided a unique opportunity for the nonprofit to strengthen relationships with each expert guest.

Community Strategic Visioning Using Meeting in a Box

I've worked with city visioning projects using a community planning "meeting in a box" approach. This is a creative technique where the facilitating organization (such as a nonprofit or a municipality) equips leaders from community-based organizations to meet with their own groups for visioning and input for a number of topics. The input is then summarized and integrated into a citywide report.

To provide community feedback in a format you can consistently collect and process, you can provide community leaders with digital files for presentations they can use, along with discussion guides that cover critical topics.

Assemble and deliver your meeting box. Include a facilitator guide, handouts, meeting ideas, and breakout exercises. A cost-effective plus: files can be duplicated and distributed using a shared drive such as a USB, with a master hard copy of all handouts also provided in each box.

CHAPTER 4

STRATEGIC PLANNING POST-COVID-19: GOING VIRTUAL

AS 2019 CAME TO AN END, "2020 Vision" became a popular mantra for looking toward the start of an epic new decade. But by late January, nothing was further from the truth. No one could have predicted the global impact of the COVID-19 pandemic of 2020. This fast-spreading virus, estimated by the Centers for Disease Control to be ten times more deadly than H1N1 influenza, impacted millions of people worldwide and cost hundreds of thousands of lives.

All forms of group gatherings were disbanded across the globe. COVID-19 spread quickly from country to country, shaking up headlines by the hour as it marched onward. Fundraisers, conferences, and social events were abruptly canceled. Leaders worldwide pleaded with people to stay home and fight the rapid spread of the virus by social distancing. Governments mandated stay-at-home policies to flatten the infection curve with the hopes of helping hospitals across the globe cope with the overrun of sick people and medical supply shortages.

It was like someone hit a global reset button. Almost overnight, university courses began instruction online and via Zoom and other similar tools. Much of the world's workforce transitioned to working from home, using online video conferencing technology.

Today, we know that virtual meeting technology has the power to bring our planning teams together and save us time, money, and expensive facility rentals. Money is saved on venues, flights, hotels, and travel expenses; there is also less setup and travel time. This can reduce impacts on the environment as well.

Prior to COVID-19, most of us in the workplace had participated in a handful of on-screen virtual conference meetings using early apps such as Zoom, FaceTime, and WhatsApp. I had used Zoom only a few times as a tool for featuring expert panelists on a virtual basis. When COVID-19 hit, I quickly learned that effective facilitation is just as important and perhaps even more imperative for creating dialogue and idea sharing for virtual meetings. It's important that facilitators make sure all participants have opportunities to contribute.

A CEO standing on stage with a microphone reading practiced lines—the classic "sage on the stage"—is an outdated model of leadership. In virtual settings, a facilitative style of "guide on the side" can help you inspire inclusive, immersive, interactive, and engaging conversations.

Box CEO Aaron Levie believes virtual meetings provide a new democratized setting where everyone is seen on the same screen, in the same-sized squares. This reduces traditional top-down organizational hierarchies and allows for a new level of transparency, creativity, inspiration, and collaboration across time zones and regions.[1]

Lessons learned from the COVID-19 pandemic will impact the culture of work for generations to come. The efficiency of working remotely from home, coupled with being able to connect through online meeting technology, will enhance strategic planning as well.

No doubt this can include hybrid combinations of in-person group strategy sessions supplemented by nimble virtual discussions and training sessions. With virtual meetings, the prohibitive costs of travel are eliminated. For multisite and international organizations, offering one or more virtual strategic planning meetings can open up opportunities for more employees to attend as well as guest speakers to be featured, creating a budget-friendly way to include a diverse mix of participants who otherwise might not be able to attend.

While there's nothing like attending a strategic planning workshop in person, you can help your organization explore virtual, conference-style meeting platforms that allow employees to move around a meeting facility, clicking from one virtual area to the next. Employees can attend keynote and breakout sessions in a virtual environment designed to make them feel like they're sitting among peers in a theater.

Employees can use their phones or tablets as a second screen for chats or Q&A sessions while watching speakers on the primary meeting screen. They can connect with other attendees for networking and discussion, connect with strategic plan resources, and go back and watch recorded sessions, available immediately and posted after the event. Virtual meeting and large-scale conferencing technology will evolve, enhancing the experience for participants who otherwise couldn't attend in person.

I encourage you to consider how your strategic planning program might be repackaged to include virtual components, such as strategy sessions. Become skilled at weaving together webinars, video conferencing and virtual panels, discussion forums, and breakout sessions.

Many organizations combine virtual meetings with well-structured offline activities, such as smaller group homework assignments. A series of meetings can be scheduled to bring the larger strategic planning group together where homework teams present findings, share on-screen presentations, and invite discussion.

In a virtual context where people's attention spans are shorter while staring at others through a screen, it will require a series of virtual meetings to host what normally might occur during a one-day meeting in person. For example, a virtual series could include an opening trends panel with guest speakers for the first session, followed by a competitive intelligence review for the second session, and a discussion about the organization's desired future and gap analysis in the third session, along with strategic goal breakout groups.

Suppose a trade association wants to benchmark five other state's associations. The steering committee might identify the five top comparison states most relevant to the association.

Five homework teams could be charged with taking the assignment offline and working together in their small group. Each team could answer a list of benchmark questions about operations, financial resources, communication strategies, and member products and services. This offline investigative work would be substantial. It could include reviewing websites, placing a call to the association's executive, and answering all questions as thoroughly as possible.

When reconvening virtually, each team could share a 20-minute presentation of the findings, followed by Q&A. This session could take up to three hours, including a few stretch breaks. The session could be recorded and a written transcript, including chat comments and questions, could be produced. This session could be one among several to bring strategic plan participants together in an interactive virtual setting.

But the key matter at stake is how leaders will be able to create rich, meaningful leadership experiences through strategic planning without physically being in the same room together. Here are a few of my recommendations.

FOCUS ON CREATING A VITAL HUMAN EXPERIENCE—NOT JUST THE TECHNOLOGY TOOLS

Vital strategic planning focuses on creating a life-changing leadership experience starting with the workshop—a shared experience that strengthens bonds throughout the organization. If you want to build engagement and connections among your participants, you (and your organization) will need to be proficient in using the technology tools to draw people together virtually, in one room. But beyond that, you will need to be skilled at fostering relationships in distributed work environments, bringing out the best in the group.

For global and multisite companies, technology allows for frequent, cost-effective meetings. As more people work remotely, virtual strategic planning techniques can minimize barriers of distance and time, build trust, and ensure a more diverse volume of idea exchange.

One key point to keep in mind is that you will have to maintain your focus on creating a vital strategic planning experience using the three-part framework—rather than on the technology tools themselves. This can be tricky, because proficiency with the tools is critical to conducting a smooth, seamless meeting. But the tools can't run the meeting for you. Only you and your attention to cultivating quality conversations can make a successful meeting happen.

Focus on discussion and decision making during your virtual meeting. Ask for input for needed decisions, and encourage use of the chat function for asking questions about the decision and voting for a decision. For smaller groups (such as fifty people or less), some organizations provide prefabricated small signs, such as "thumbs up" for quickly providing feedback like agreement and approval, or a question mark if there's confusion, or a company logo in a star for symbolizing celebration.

These small signs can be e-mailed to all participants for optional use. This can add an element of fun and visual expression.

For virtual strategic planning meetings, leaders can create a spirit of teamwork by arriving to the virtual meeting room 10 minutes early and inviting a bit of brief storytelling as people are joining each meeting. Ask about the photo in the background on their desk or cabinet. Have someone give you a tour of their office. Invite everyone to grab a coffee before you start.[2]

Virtual meetings should begin on time, as planned. Try a warm-up topic for the first five minutes, such as asking a participant or two to share a current strategic issue or trend that has occurred since the last conversation. This warm-up activity can engage the group and help participants move into a strategic frame of mind.

Increase understanding of your strategic planning process by using visual tools. Use a program road map showing the process of your organization's strategic planning process, as well as a strategic plan leadership map showing how vision, mission, strategic pillars, strategic goals, and department goals tie together—and how goals help to deliver on the organization's vision and mission.

ENCOURAGE SOCIAL CONNECTIONS

Successful virtual strategic planning encourages a shared discovery process. This creates a "with" mindset, not a "top-down, power-over-you" meeting style where the facilitator or executive is viewed as an authority figure. That is, with products such as Zoom, Webex, and GoToMeeting, everyone appears equally in a small box on the screen, creating a sense that everyone is on the same team. There are no larger and smaller boxes, nor is there hierarchy in how the boxes appear on the screen. This can create a more participative virtual meeting environment where there's potential for everyone to be seen and heard unfiltered, and on a level playing field.

Be intentional about encouraging social connections. As an easy and interesting conversation starter, use your meeting technology *prior* to the meeting by setting up a virtual poll. Your poll could be focused on purely a fun topic such as a multiple-choice question about people's favorite hobby or food, or it could be work related.

Polls provide an easy, confidential way to create an opening warmup activity. You can invite opinion sharing and prioritize strategies, ideas, and other content. Questions can be interesting and informative, such as:

- Where are you joining us from? (open-ended)

- What would you like to learn today? (provide three to five choices)

- In one word, how would you describe the next years for our company? (open-ended)

- Which of the following trends do you think will impact our company the most? (provide three to five trends for multiple choice)

Put the human experience first—building trust, engagement, and connections among the participants is very important. One executive I know uses a simple, one-word opening and closing exercise to check in with her staff. Your question could be focused on the strategic planning meeting, such as: What is the one word that comes to mind when you think of the word "change"? Or it could be an easy personal question with a one- or two-word answer, such as: Who is your hero right now?

To be effective, virtual meeting facilitation should be just as focused and engaging as in-person meetings—maybe even more so. Rich conversations help us make sense of the world so that we can take appropriate action. These are important in virtual settings, just as they are in face-to-face meetings. But accomplishing this will likely take more time and effort to achieve virtually, and may require more facilitator and group patience.

PREPARE TO COACH YOUR PARTICIPANTS

At the start of the meeting, review the agenda and meeting objectives, as well as a few ground rules for norms. You may need to provide a bit of coaching for participants about how to show up, using the "lights, camera, and action" checklist. First, the lights: there must be enough light on each participant's face so that everybody can be clearly seen. Second, the camera: the computer camera must be close enough to each person's face to show expression. This provides the sense of being in the same room. Each person needs to be clearly seen and heard. Each person should look into the camera lens when speaking to enhance eye-to-eye contact. Third, the action: participants should aim to keep their on-camera backgrounds free from distractions and movement during the strategic planning meeting. This same checklist applies to the facilitator, whether it's you or someone else.

Other topics about which you may need to coach include the process for raising hands and providing input without speaking over other participants. Throughout your virtual strategic plan workshop, seek opportunities to create common language around planning terminology to overcome jargon. Build shared understanding around terms such as "environmental scan," the act of collecting data external to the organization to help guide decisions about the organization's strategic direction.

As the virtual meeting leader, you and your company leaders can create a safe space for authentic, secure, and confidential conversations. Always inform your participants if any part of the online virtual meeting will be recorded. Never record a session without first telling your participants that the meeting will be recorded, whether for archival purposes or for showing to those who were unable to attend.

TEACH YOUR TEAM MEMBERS ABOUT THE TECHNOLOGY

Embrace the human emotion of fear when leveraging technology for virtual strategic planning. If an individual or group is scared, then work through the fear. As strategic planning virtual meeting technology evolves, I'm assuming that my following points will continue to be relevant.

Plan a practice session for those who would like to learn how to use your virtual meeting tool. Explain how to use features such as screen view options, chat, hand-raising, breakout groups, and polling. Minimize the risk of technology issues distracting from your meeting content. Ask a colleague to monitor chat throughout the virtual meeting to answer technology issues. Take technology issues out of chat and offline as soon as possible, so that your chat function does not become the help desk.[3]

During a virtual strategic planning meeting with a nonprofit board, I was able to organize a prestigious expert panel with three speakers who attended by Zoom. These are busy executives who otherwise would not have been able to travel. Instead, they appeared together on a large screen. One of the panelists had never used virtual meeting technology. It was important to conduct a practice call to increase the panelist's comfort with the technology. The panel went off without a hitch.

With virtual meetings, it's important to manage expectations. Keep in mind that it's the *quality* of the thinking and engagement that is important. Helping others to understand and appreciate this is important, so that they accept the virtual meeting process in spite of any perceived difficulties with using the technology.

BUILD PRE-MEETING READINESS: WHAT GETS SHOWN AND DISCUSSED

Pre-meeting readiness is vital to building small-group teamwork and to enhancing the quality of conversation during your virtual planning meetings. For virtual meetings, the most important pre-meeting planning decisions you'll make involve selecting what gets shown and discussed. Your virtual meeting time is limited and extremely valuable, and must be treated with the same pristine time management as in-person meetings to keep topics and people on track.

Connect with your contributors prior to individual planning meetings to ensure they are ready to share information. To avoid putting people on the spot, provide some advance notice to participants if you expect to call on them to share important information that may need advance preparation or thinking time.

People absorb knowledge using different methods of learning, and we perceive information using our senses. The three most practical senses in learning environments are sight (visual), hearing (auditory), and touch (kinesthetic). With meeting tools such as Zoom, your activities can include interesting visuals. All materials must be reviewed and tailored to what participants can grasp. For example, small, difficult-to-read charts will need to be simplified and enlarged for readability.

The chat function can engage those whose learning styles are visual. For auditory learners, you can create listening activities and breakout discussions. Virtual whiteboard, digital polling with the click of the mouse, and writing activities can activate the sense of touch.

But you'll have to put some of yourself into this advance planning to develop interesting and fun activities. If an activity does not go quite as planned, give yourself permission to reboot or redirect the activity. If needed, simply ask for your audience's patience. A bit of humor can humanize operator error and smooth over technical difficulties. While some planners think that the traditional use of paper flip charts, Post-it notes, and sticky dots for voting are outdated, I still like these for in-person meetings. In a virtual setting, you can find a number of collaboration technology tools featuring similar flip-chart and voting techniques. These provide great options for enhancing visual interest and opinion sharing.

Virtual Flip Charts and Whiteboards

Post-it flip charts are one of my favorite in-person meeting tools. Individual sheets can be easily moved, rearranged, and posted on a variety of walls. Here are three great features of Post-it flip charts. First, there's no need for bulky flip-chart stands. Second, these adhesive flip charts add great flexibility for moving information around to various wall locations as needed. Third, there's no worry about using messy tape and damaging walls. Traditional flip-chart activities get people moving around a room.

The flexibility to reposition flip charts adds sophistication to the meeting. While Post-it flip charts are a bit more expensive, I think the extra cost is worth every penny.

For conducting virtual meetings, there are a growing number of digital whiteboard tools such as Miro. While physical flip charts and whiteboards are based on size, they are not limited this way digitally. Cloud apps allow easy collaboration with other users where comments can be added. Files can be shared across devices. Links, images, and other files can be attached for easy reference.

Virtual mind-mapping tools such as Conceptboard can be very helpful to you for vision and mission brainstorming activities. Ideas can be shared simultaneously when everyone adds their ideas on sticky notes in real time.

STICKY DOTS AND VOTING: FUN IN PERSON (INCLUDING VIRTUAL MEETINGS)

After any type of strategy session or brainstorm where ideas are canvassed, colored sticky dots are the perfect tool for group voting as a follow-up exercise to prioritize input.

For virtual strategic planning or hybrid sessions, there are several online tools such as PollUnit that replicate dot voting, or "dotmocracy," in online polling formats. Some offer free voting for up to a certain number of participants.

For either virtual or in-person workshop sessions, after your strategy discussions where recommendations have been documented, give participants a reasonable number of dots (around twenty), and ask them to prioritize or support top strategic plan initiatives that have been written on flip charts.

Each person will vote by tacking one or more dots next to an idea or strategic goal. Encourage the group to vote independently. As noted in the previous chapter, I recommend that you set a limit of not more than three dots posted on any given item to avoid having anyone use all of their votes on one or two of their favorite strategic initiatives to gain unfair advantage for their favorite goal. At the end of the voting exercise, participants will see which success strategies receive the most support. Strategic plan three-year goals will be prioritized by the number of individual sticky dots placed on the list of success strategies.

No Getting Out of Pre-Meeting Homework

Just as you do for in-person pre-meeting homework assignments, you can assign homework to your teams and ask them to be ready to present their findings. Teams can tackle what otherwise would be enormous consultants' projects such as competitive intelligence, SWOT and PESTEL analysis, industry trends reports, or a summary recap of survey findings such as customer, employee, donor, and investor surveys. Request your teams to send digital presentations and visual tools (PowerPoint slides, for example) at least one day prior to your strategic planning workshop.

For example, a trade association wanted to benchmark its programs and services based on other regional trade associations. The board of directors divided into four teams. Each team answered the same list of homework questions. Questions focused on the types of programs and services, how these are promoted, the program and service cost, and the ease of registering for programs.

Their presentations revealed best practices for membership benefits, program variety, and use of webinars as ways to grow membership value. Board members were surprised to see a few common themes that pointed to their own association's service gaps and new opportunities.

You, the virtual workshop curator, will need to make sure you have done your pre-meeting homework too. You'll need to review all your materials in advance to make sure they are properly prepared for screen sharing.

A lesson I quickly learned was that it's a bit embarrassing to be showing your screen to a large audience while you're hustling to find files during the meeting. Train yourself to open all files in advance. And as you're searching for the next presentation, be sure your "screen share" function is turned off!

Assign the Pre-Meeting Reading

Just as you do for in-person reading assignments, send important reading materials to your participants two to four weeks prior to your virtual strategic planning workshop. A brief summary of your organization's business environment is the first thing you should send to all participants, including executive management. You could include a simple worksheet where they can actively take notes and answer a few relevant questions. Ask them to be ready to share insights about key topics.

Examples of helpful pre-meeting reading can include articles about external trends and business environment information impacting the organization. This could include a best-selling business book providing novel business or leadership ideas, current published academic journal research providing an in-depth look at your industry, or news articles featuring competitors launching innovative new products.

Do Your Own Homework

Your organization's own homework might involve pre-meeting research, data collecting, or polling. Some pre-workshop activities, such as quantitative and qualitative market research, are best suited for the experts in your organization who know how to properly conduct surveys, focus groups, online interviews, phone surveys, and social media market research. If an organization lacks internal expertise, external marketing firms may enhance the ability to collect, analyze, and summarize data important to the business. A feasibility study is a great market research option for businesses looking to open a new location or start a new business. Research such as customer service surveys can be completed through e-mail or an online link share.

A national egg producer wanted to understand consumer purchasing decisions and attitudes toward eggs. The required research work went well beyond the egg producer's staff's expertise. A market research firm was hired, and more than one thousand surveys were mailed and returned. The research was targeted to household grocery shoppers over age twenty-five who made purchasing decisions.

The following questions were asked, and the resulting data was presented at the company's strategic planning opening session. This data guided the executive team's strategy decisions for operations and marketing:

- What egg brands are shoppers aware of?

- How satisfied are consumers with the egg producer?

- How often do consumers purchase the egg producer's brand?

- What other factors are important when buyers are purchasing eggs?

- Are shoppers aware of advertising for the producer?

- What are current consumer egg use habits?

- What new trends are on the horizon for general grocery shopping?

INCORPORATE VIRTUAL EXPERT SPEAKERS AND PANELISTS

Virtual participation, for all of its potential challenges, offers an easy solution for limited speaker and travel budgets. I've included board members via Zoom who otherwise would not have been able to attend a strategic planning meeting. I've also featured an impressive array of high-profile speakers who normally would not be able to join an in-person strategic planning workshop. Another way to add life and vitality to a virtual workshop is to host a panel. I recommend no more than four, maybe five speakers—as you would do for an in-person panel—to allow ample time for each speaker to share ideas.

The key to facilitating an effective in-person panel is prepanel communication. I recommend sending individual invitations—an e-mail followed by a letter invitation if a formal invitation is needed—asking your desired panelists to participate. You'll want to state the purpose of the panel and a few potential topics and questions that you would be interested in having discussed.

Once you have your panelists confirmed, I like to follow up and thank them by sending one or more group e-mails to confirm the group as a whole, so that the panelists can see who else is participating. This creates an esprit de corps among the panelists, and it can often lead to future collaboration and lifelong friendships following the workshop. After all, we want this to be a life-changing experience, and this is one of the ways this can happen.

HELP YOUR BOARD MEMBERS STAY ENGAGED

McKinsey conducted a survey of nearly 1,600 corporate boards of directors.[4] A shocking finding revealed that only 10 percent of those board members said they actually understood the industry dynamics, such as the competitive environment in which their companies operated. Consequently, only 21 percent understood their organization's strategies. The surprising data explained the disconnect between corporate board members and their lack of strategy involvement with the companies they represented.

The McKinsey data has strategy implications for all boards, including those for nonprofit and trade associations. Your virtual strategic planning program can play an instrumental role in educating board members about industry trends and competitive threats.

Virtual meeting technology can enable busy board members to participate in not only steering committees, but also in strategic planning workshops in situations where in-person attendance wouldn't be possible. By virtually involving your board of directors in the creation of your organization's strategic plan, your executive team can go the extra mile and ensure the board is immersed in industry trends and fully understands the strategic direction.

McKinsey asked three excellent, timeless questions that you can also use to candidly explore issues with your organization's executive team and board members:

1. Do board members understand the organization's industry's dynamics?

2. Has there been enough board–management debate before a specific strategy is discussed?

3. Have the board and management discussed all strategic options and wrestled them to the ground?

Whether virtually or in person, I recommend that your organization review strategic plan progress and summarize updates no less than quarterly, with an annual report at the end of your organization's fiscal year. Digital dashboards, scorecards, and animated infographics can enhance your ongoing virtual reports and presentations.

Without a doubt, virtual meeting technology will continue to be one of the fastest-growing industry sectors. During COVID-19, subscriptions to digital meeting platforms skyrocketed overnight. Companies have found that the online meeting technology is easy to use and that it does a great job linking employees together while reducing travel and meeting costs.

Make sure to find a virtual meeting platform that works well for your organization's structure and culture, and allows breakout groups and employs strategic dialogues the same way you would do in person. There are ways to brainstorm in small groups where everyone can contribute and synthesize ideas, and virtual planning sessions have the ability to feature chat, which captures comments and ideas in the chat box, allowing everyone to see their contribution in real time and share them afterward.

Virtual Strategic Planning Tools

The list of virtual meeting and planning tools is ever growing, so I won't make an attempt to provide a definitive list, as this admittedly will become outdated.

The following companies were among some of the earliest entrants offering cloud-based strategic planning meeting and collaboration tools prior to and during the COVID-19 pandemic.* Virtual meeting and file-sharing services were in high demand, including video conferencing, online meetings, team messaging, screen share, webinars, web conferencing, and cloud calling.

- **Cisco's Webex** is a cloud-based suite of productivity tools that keeps teams connected. Including Webex Teams, Webex Meetings, and Webex Devices.

- **Google Hangouts** is a communication software product developed by Google. Originally a feature of Google+, Hangouts became

continued

a stand-alone product in 2013. In 2017, Google began developing Hangouts into a product aimed at enterprise communication. Hangouts is now part of the G Suite line of products and consists of two primary products: Google Meet and Google Chat.

- **GoToMeeting** is an online meeting, desktop sharing, and video conferencing software package that enables the user to meet with other computer users, customers, clients, or colleagues in real time.

- **Microsoft Teams** is a unified communication and collaboration platform that combines persistent workplace chat, video meetings, file storage, and application integration.

- **Zoom** is a meeting and classroom platform designed to provide clear images of multiple participants (up to a hundred with the Pro version), with easy transfer of screen control.

Virtual Co-Creating and Team Idea-Generating Tools

- **Adobe Connect** is software used to create information and general presentations, online training materials, web conferencing, learning modules, webinars, and user desktop sharing. All meeting rooms are organized into "pods," with each pod performing a specific role.

- **Conceptboard** is a centralized hub for content and ideas supporting remote teams in collaborating across time zones. The tool is especially useful for visual collaboration.

- **Crowdsourcing technology** is being used in new strategic planning contexts such as idea generating. This technology can be used as a voting tool, providing accurate data with less potential for bias and more rigor applied to prioritization of strategy recommendations.

- **Force Field Analysis** is a framework for analyzing and responding to the positive and negative factors that impact a business situation, strategic issue, or business opportunity. There are a variety of online tools supporting this framework.

- **Futures Platform**™ is an online tool incorporating strategic foresight to explore future trends and drivers of change to identify opportunities and risks to support strategy development, risk management, innovation and R&D, and other situations where validated future content is needed. Strategic foresight is a planning-oriented discipline related to futures studies, the study of the future. In a business context, a more action-oriented approach has become well-known as corporate foresight.

- **GroupMind** is a collective intelligence software allowing virtual idea generation and prioritization, group discussion, as well as alignment and buy-in to the strategic plan.

- **Howspace** is an artificial intelligence (AI)–based platform that allows users to collaborate in professional learning and company training initiatives.

- **Immersive Terf**® is a 3D immersive environment for meetings and decision making. It's a virtual place where people meet, engage, and create in a secure environment. Each user is represented by an avatar and controls their own experience, with navigation and tools for content sharing and creation. Participants can share documents and chat, and use a whiteboard, sticky notes, live video, screen share, and streaming video. Virtual locations resemble actual physical rooms. These provide a sense of continuity and help participants pick up where they left off.

- **InsightVision** is an online strategy management platform enabling strategies to be developed, refined, measured, and monitored online. Strategies for big issues require many meetings, each only advancing a small part of the larger strategy where strategy management is needed.

- **Mind mapping tools, such as MindView and MindManager,** feature professional mind-mapping software that allows participants to visually brainstorm, organize, and present ideas. MindManager, developed by Mindjet, provides ways for users to visualize information

continued

in mind maps and flowcharts. Similar to a virtual whiteboard, it lets users capture ideas and information, then organize and contextualize the information for managing projects, organizing information, and brainstorming.

• **Miro** is an online whiteboard collaborative platform. It provides ideation and brainstorming software with a zoomable canvas and web whiteboard, enabling participants to add input, plan projects from all angles, and create centralized hubs of information, seeing both the big picture and details.

• **SchellingPoint** provides organizations and consultants with digital technology and collaboration methodology for designing strategies, transformations, mergers, innovations, policies, and projects.

• **ThinkPoints** is a strategy development tool designed for a distributed workforce. It offers virtual whiteboards and provides a digital record of ideas and group sharing. Participants develop new strategies or pivot current ones and then cascade these through their organization.

• **World Café, also known as Knowledge Café**, is a structured conversational process for knowledge sharing, relationship building, and making sense of a complex, ever-changing world. Groups of people can meet virtually as well as in person to discuss a topic at several small tables like those in a café. The aim is to maximize time spent in conversation and limit time spent with one person presenting. Although predefined questions may have been agreed upon at the beginning, outcomes or solutions are not decided in advance. The assumption is that collective discussion can shift people's conceptions and encourage collective action.

Virtual Project Management Tools

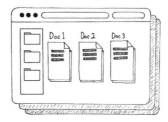

- **AchieveIt** is a software platform designed for large organizations to get their biggest, most important initiatives into a company-wide view, engaging employees for accountability,

- **Cascade Strategy** is software that takes a plan, manage, and track approach with the aim to include the entire workforce in an inclusive process. Each part of the plan-manage-track model includes support steps.

- **ClearPoint Strategy** provides a cloud-based strategic planning execution and tracking to align and update organizational goals, measures, projects, and tasks. It provides visual and interactive tracking reports from the enterprise level to the individual performance level.

- **Monday.com and Slack** are online workflow management tools allowing virtual work forces to plan, run, and track remote work projects.

- **Workfront** is an enterprise project management software platform. With Workfront, teams receive requests in a standard format, and managers prioritize incoming projects, make assignments, and receive project reports.

Virtual Information Sharing Tools
and Online Records Repositories

- **Box** is a global cloud content management platform founded in 2005 for file sharing and is a secure, second-storage system to support

continued

workplace collaboration. Box simplifies work for organizations from one location to many, as well as distributed, virtual work. Box assists companies with automating repeatable workflows, such as company onboarding and storage of contracts and digital files.

- **Google Docs** is an application allowing users to create and edit files online while collaborating with other users in real time. Edits are tracked by a user with a revision history presenting changes. An editor's position is highlighted with an editor-specific color and cursor. A permissions system regulates what users can do.

- **Wikis are composition systems.** A wiki is a knowledge-based website on which users collaboratively modify and structure content directly from a web browser. In a typical wiki, text is written using a simplified markup language and often edited with the help of a rich-text editor. A collaborative company wiki is run using wiki software, otherwise known as a wiki engine.

* Association for Strategic Planning 2020b.

CHAPTER 5

YOUR VITAL WRITTEN PLAN: THE SHARED STORY OF STRATEGIC INTENT

STRATEGIC PLANS TRADITIONALLY HAVE BEEN COMPLICATED, boring, and difficult for employees to understand—anything but vital, in fact. The traditional written plans of the past were destined to become shelf ornaments because they were created by a tight circle of top-down executives, and the material in them was difficult to read.

In today's digital world, where attention spans are shrinking, your strategic plan must be clear and compelling, and it must be easy to read and easy to understand by the 96 percent of leaders who are *non*strategists.[1]

The hallmarks of a *vital* written plan include being meaningful, valuable, effectively communicated, digital, accessible, interactive, personal, accountable, promoted, and maybe even *fun.* Your written plan can be produced as a hard-copy document, but it also can be a digital document you can share on your organization's website and economically send through electronic and social media distribution with links added for a deeper dive into detailed data, background, maps, and charts.

In today's digital world, influencers have mastered the art of telling personal stories, and some are paid handsomely for their skill and visibility. In fact, 55 percent of business professionals say that a great story captures their focus and keeps them engaged with content.[2] Humans learn from stories. In addition to featuring your vital strategic goals, your plan should involve specific stories that spotlight the organization's people, departments, and vital work.

A technology trade association includes a brief summary of its strategic plan into the organization's annual report. This embedded strategic plan is cleverly designed on two pages. It features strategic initiatives and the organization's vision, mission, and values. Each strategic initiative showcases innovation and notes the staff and board member accountable for progress.

This publication features a "Who's Who" of the state's major technology and innovation companies as well as members, boards, and committees. The annual report is distributed to a significant VIP list including several thousand association members, elected officials, and economic development leaders.

In addition to adding stories, you'll want to address the fact that more than 80 percent of business professionals said the use of animated visuals in presentations is effective in increasing their audience engagement.[3]

As attention spans are shorter than ever before, you'll want to respond to the increasing need to present strategic planning data in brief and visually new ways. Ninety-five percent of all business professionals say they do or have multitasked at some point during the meetings they attend. Even during live company presentations, at least eight out of ten attendees shift their focus away from the speaker at some point during the meeting—often to look at their phones.[4] This is just one more reason you have to be judicious about the ways you choose to present your material.

Your strategic plan can help your organization become a beacon of light as well as a global sensation for good, making our world a better place.

WHAT SHOULD YOUR VITAL WRITTEN PLAN ACCOMPLISH?

This chapter will help you focus on the strategic content of your plan with confidence and remove the stress of overthinking the format. Whether you decide to write the strategic plan yourself or hire an expert writer, the easy-to-use outline that follows will help you and your team create a compelling, visionary road map for your organization's success.

An engaging written strategic plan will help your organization achieve the following objectives:

- Present and explain strategic goals, usually covering a three-year time frame.

- Ensure all of your strategic goals fit the acronym of SMART—Specific, Measurable, Attainable, Results-oriented, and Time-Based.

- Show how strategic goals cascade from the top to the bottom of the organization and how departments align both vertically and horizontally between each other.

- Connect your organization's annual operating plan to longer-term strategies. For each strategic goal, it will clearly define what will be accomplished during the year ahead. These twelve-month goals define your organization's annual operating plan.

- Help the organization's employees understand how their personal goals connect to department and company goals.

- Describe how goals will be tracked, communicated, and celebrated. Your tracking system can provide a systematic, visual approach to linking strategic goals.

An engaging strategic plan is an accessible one, produced in *both* written and digital formats. The digital version can be promoted on websites, e-mail "e-blasts," and through social media. Digital promotion should be brief and eye-catching. Include interesting charts, infographics, and brief videos to explain key points. Offer links for a deeper dive into company background and supporting materials.

- To pique readers' attention, use well-designed infographics to provide a snapshot of your organization's exciting future. If you need to jump-start ideas, many examples of strategic planning infographics are available online by searching for "strategic plan infographics."

YOUR VITAL WRITTEN STRATEGIC PLAN FRAMEWORK

For your written strategic plan, you can customize this easy-to-use framework to fit your organization's needs. Then, if you desire, you can hire a skilled writer to edit and polish your final draft.

1. CEO or Board Chairman Introduction Letter

Introduce your plan with an introduction letter. While some organizations may prefer to avoid "outdating" the strategic plan by featuring the current CEO and board leaders in the event leadership changes, employees and external audiences such as customers, shareholders, and donors appreciate seeing who on the executive team has a commitment to the plan. This is the place for an authentic, inspirational message from a leader in the organization providing a visionary view and their endorsement of the strategic plan.

2. Executive Summary

Your organization can increase readership and impact of your strategic plan by creating an executive summary. You or your assigned writer will identify the plan's key points, including the pillars and strategic goal priorities for each pillar, and will develop a well-crafted opening executive summary. This one- to two-page summary should be able to stand alone as an exciting short story. Your executive summary could be packaged into a brochure, a website feature, blog post, and slip sheet that can be used for a variety of internal and external communication purposes. The content also could be parsed into a social media series.

The summary's job is to provide a succinct overview of your written strategic plan. It should share your most important inspirational strategic goals and initiatives as well as industry challenges. If you do not feature a CEO or board chairman letter, you will want to invite your top executives to sign the executive summary to spotlight executive commitment.

3. Vision or Grand Purpose, Mission, Values, and History

In this section, you will share your organization's guiding principles by adding the following pieces.

Vision Statement

Include the organization's vision statement, which describes the aspirational future horizon where the organization is headed. In recent years, many organizations also have developed an overarching "grand purpose statement" describing how the organization intends to profoundly impact the world. This statement should also be included in this section. For example, Apple's vision is "We believe that we are on the face of the earth to make great products, and that's not changing."[5] This is an aspirational statement of a futuristic and general nature.

Mission Statement

Add the organization's mission statement next. This statement presents what the organization does and in some cases, why and how the organization does it. Apple's mission is "bringing the best user experience to its customers through its innovative hardware, software, and services."[6] In contrast to their vision statement, this description is more specific and focuses on the organization's cause and what it provides or *does*.

Most mission statements fall between two and four sentences in length and are not more than one hundred words in all. Your organization's mission statement should be just the right length to get the point across, and it should be designed to be an internal document that explains how the organization inspires your team to achieve the company goals.[7] Short vision and mission statements are often the most powerful and memorable. These feature carefully chosen words that succinctly describe the organization's aspirational purpose and body of work. For example, TED has a poignant two-word mission statement: "spread ideas."[8]

Values or Principles

If your company has identified guiding values or principles, add those here. Many organizations share values in the strategic plan, on the organization's website, and in the investor relations and other materials.

An organization's values are the beliefs, philosophies, and principles that drive your business. They impact the employee experience you deliver as well as the relationship you develop with your customers, partners, and shareholders. Company values are employee and customer-centric and help boost employee motivation, morale, and employee advocacy, as well as providing guidance for employee behavior in the workplace.[9]

Many organizations provide values plus vivid definitions that fully explain each value. Apple's values include "Accessibility, Education, Environment, Inclusion and Diversity, Privacy, and Supplier Responsibility."[10] Apple's website includes a separate landing page for each value, where each value is explained with extensive detail.

Cars.com describes the company's value on the "career" website page.[11] These include "Be Bold," "Start With the Consumer," "Stay Open," and "Challenge and Collaborate." This list includes definitions for each value, and helps Cars.com job applicants assess whether they can align with the company's stated character. Vivid company values also can provide an inspirational opening chapter to preface your strategic plan.

Company History

Provide a brief synopsis of your company's history in four to six paragraphs. Include historic milestones and add a visual timeline. In your digital version of the strategic plan, you can provide links to more extensive history and interesting stories.

Succinct, Powerful Mission Statements

Uber: We ignite opportunity by setting the world in motion.

Google: To organize the world's information and make it universally accessible and useful.

Kickstarter: To help bring creative projects to life.

Tesla: To accelerate the advent of sustainable transport by bringing compelling mass market electric cars to market as soon as possible.

Microsoft: To empower every person and every organization on the planet to achieve more.

Starbucks: To inspire and nurture the human spirit—one person, one cup and one neighborhood at a time.

LinkedIn: Connect the world's professionals to make them more productive and successful.

4. External Analysis

Next, present findings from your team's external analysis, which should include important findings from the homework shared at your strategic planning workshop. This section should summarize your organization's "macro environment," including industry, economic and sociopolitical trends, competition, and new or anticipated regulations and laws.

When possible, use infographics and at-a-glance charts to spotlight the findings. You will want to use this as an opportunity to expand your organization's mission impact by revealing competitive forces, pressure points, and customer needs, as well as new and emerging opportunities to serve clients.

5. Internal Analysis

Here you will want to summarize your organization's "micro environment," or the current state of its internal operations. This section will provider an insider's view of your organization. Include the key findings from the internal assessments that were discussed at your strategic planning workshop. This is where you can include workshop reports such as those that follow.

- **SWOT analysis:** Your organization's strengths, weaknesses, opportunities, and threats.

- **Gap analysis:** A review of where your organization is now, where it needs to be, and any existing gaps.

- **A summary of stakeholder survey results:** Survey research could be conducted a month or two prior to your strategic planning workshop. This internal analysis would be considered as pre-workshop research. Stakeholders or constituents could include anyone with interest in your organization, including customers, members, employees, alumni, suppliers, and any relevant audience group.

6. Four Pillars and Strategic Goals

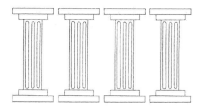

Now it's time to introduce your organization's strategic pillars: your organization's four distinct support systems that provide stability and support your firm's future growth opportunities. These are the large-scope and most critical functions common to *all* organizations, whether they are for-profit, nonprofit, or governmental in structure.

Your strategic plan will describe your organization's four pillars and a set of prioritized strategic goals to advance each pillar. For each pillar, your strategic plan should list your strategic goals in priority order, based on the outcomes of your strategic planning workshop discussions.

Pillar 1: Programs, Products, and Services

The Programs, Products, and Services pillar describes your organization's tangible products and the services it provides to customers to meet their needs and wants. All tangible products include some element of customer service embedded in delivery and support for the product.

For example, computers, cars, clothes, phones, and furniture are tangible products, and all require service by employees who support customers with empathy, active listening, and deep product knowledge. Service creates happy customers, and this can lead to customer retention, repeat sales, and referrals to new customers.

Some organizations, such as those providing behavioral health counseling or healthcare, feature programs and services. That is, the "products" are the range of programs and services provided to the "customer" or client.

Pillar 2: Financial

The Financial pillar presents a detailed overview of the revenue sources that fuel your organization or business. Revenue is the total amount of income generated by the sale of goods or services related to your organization's primary operations.

The revenue number is the income a company or nonprofit organization generates before any expenses are taken out. A revenue stream is a distinct source of income, including sales of physical or digital products, service fees, subscriptions, data access fees, license fees, and other types of income.

Pillar 3: Operational Effectiveness

The Operational Effectiveness pillar addresses your organization's internal operational effectiveness. This includes administrative support functions, such as payroll, information technology, human resources, employee learning and training, continuing education programs, and supply chain activities. Operations is the work of managing the inner workings of any organization, whether business, nonprofit, or trade association. The pillar is important because operations management creates efficiency within an organization behind the scenes, in order to maximize the profit or resource management of an organization.

Pillar 4: External Outreach
(Communication, Marketing, and Branding)

This External Outreach pillar illustrates your organization's external outreach priorities and activities. These encompass communication, marketing, branding, and many types of promotional initiatives, community relations, media relations, and public relations, and all forms of digital and social media outreach.

Strategic Goals for Each Pillar

Once you have described each of your organization's strategic pillars, you will want to list the top-priority strategic goals supporting the individual pillars.

During the past few decades, the SMART acronym has expanded to include other variations, as noted here:

S	specific, significant, stretching
M	measurable, meaningful, motivational
A	attainable, achievable, agreed-upon, acceptable, actionable, action-oriented
R	realistic, relevant, reasonable, rewarding, results-oriented
T	time-based, time-bound, time-framed, timely, tangible, trackable

But to keep it simple for your organization, I recommend that you avoid acronym fads. My personal favorite description of SMART is: **s**pecific, **m**easurable, **a**ttainable, **r**esults-oriented, and **t**ime-bound.

For your written plan, use these pillar headings, followed by the strategic goals listed in priority order based on the ranking discussed at the workshop:

• **PROGRAMS, PRODUCTS, AND SERVICES**
◦ Strategic Goal 1
◦ Strategic Goal 2
◦ Etc.
• **FINANCIAL**
◦ Strategic Goal 1
◦ Strategic Goal 2
◦ Etc.
• **OPERATIONAL EFFECTIVENESS**
◦ Strategic Goal 1
◦ Strategic Goal 2
◦ Etc.
• **EXTERNAL OUTREACH (COMMUNICATION, MARKETING, AND BRANDING)**
◦ Strategic Goal 1
◦ Strategic Goal 2
◦ Etc.

7. Strategic Plan Implementation: Tracking and Communication

Most written strategic plans do not describe how goals will be implemented, communicated, and tracked. But a truly vital strategic plan will share plans for tracking and communicating progress. In this final section of your written strategic plan, you will briefly describe the process that will be used for tracking progress, communicating results, and celebrating successes.

———

FOLLOWING UP THE WORKSHOP:
THE ANNUAL OPERATING GOAL-SETTING
PROCESS AT A HIGH LEVEL

Once your organization's written strategic plan has been shaped and the strategic, three-year goals have been defined, your most important task should now focus on what the organization will ideally accomplish during the next twelve months. This means you will create a separate document to cover the goals for this time frame. These twelve-month goals will comprise the annual operating plan.

Your organization's twelve-month goals at the enterprise level will be cascaded from the executive level to all departments, company units, and employees. Effective strategic planning can incorporate a participative approach, seeking ideas from employees regarding what work group goals should be. However, to kick off this process following the strategic planning workshop, your organization's executive team must commission the work of goal setting throughout the organization, endorsing the program and leading by example.

This operating goal setting typically requires additional follow-up meetings with your organization's executive staff, together with mid-level managers and first-line supervisors in departments accountable for achieving goals for each pillar.

Each strategic goal (remember those prioritized, three-year goals supporting each pillar?) will be assigned to the managers whose staff are responsible for the corresponding functions. Each strategic goal will note the top executive or executive team accountable if certain goals have shared accountability. If the organization is small, the executive team will focus on breaking the strategic goals into annual operating goals. These are very important drill-down sessions.

The time needed to shape annual goals will vary depending on the size of your organization. After your organization's strategic goals are finalized, set up a management meeting where the strategic goals are presented. Ask each executive goal owner to meet with the appropriate group of managers and employees to shape the twelve-month goals corresponding to their strategic goals.

Set a tight but reasonable deadline for each department or unit leader to meet with their employees, draft the unit's annual goals, and submit the goals to the accountable executive for review. For workgroup level goal setting, I've found that a two-week turnaround time is reasonable for most organizations. Ask work groups to develop their unit's annual operational goals in order, according to the strategic goal's priority as determined at your strategic planning workshop.

How to Shape Annual Operating Goals

For each strategic goal being discussed, ask your executive team this question: What needs to be accomplished in the *next twelve months*? Make your operating goals SMART. Remember, the most important difference between a strategic goal and an operational goal is its *time frame*. Operational goals are short-term goals—usually twelve-month or fiscal year in time span—while strategic goals are longer-term goals extending beyond one year.

Each annual operating goal will support a strategic goal and should clearly show:

- Which strategic goal it helps to meet.

- Measurable outcomes for each annual goal. For example, if the strategic goal is to increase membership by 5 percent year over year, the annual goal for the first ten months could share a specific number of new members to recruit to reach 5 percent, such as a hundred new members. Specific annual goals should be quantified and tracked.

- Time frame: the annual goal is assumed to be a twelve-month time period corresponding with an organization's fiscal year.

- Cost: any budget associated with achieving the annual goal should be noted briefly in a column on the goal sheet and, if needed, more detailed budget information can be noted in a separate budget support document.

- Who will be held responsible? One or more executives should be noted as accountable for each pillar, with each strategic goal owner noted on the strategic goal document. The operational goal document will then note which department or division managers are accountable for the annual operating goals. (Then, for larger organizations, the company's annual goals will be cascaded down to department-level work plans.)

Do not aim for writing the "perfect goal." Aim for SMART goals that are focused on advancing progress for and achieving the corresponding three-year strategic goal.

You will want to keep written documents and on-screen presentations as simple and visually clear as possible when showing how annual, twelve-month operating goals connect with strategic goals. For a vital plan, avoid old-school planning jargon! Most employees don't know—nor do they care—about the difference between a goal or objective. Help your executive and management team keep it simple.

Use the term "strategic goal" to describe your organization's three-year goals. Then, use the term "annual operating goals" to denote twelve-month goals. Later you will help the management team work with employees to develop specific actions steps at the individual level—tactics needed to achieve the annual goals. Managers will put a deadline on each action step.

For example:

- **Strategic goal:** Achieve 10 percent sales growth year over year for the next three years.

- **Annual operating goal:** By January 1, launch the XYZ sales campaign and achieve 10 percent sales growth in year one.

- **Tactic or action step:** By January 15, hire a digital and social media marketing strategist to work directly with the sales team to support outreach to new target audiences.

Annual operating goals can be measured as frequently as your executive team desires and their tracking system permits. Most companies measure monthly progress and report quarterly results to the board of directors, followed by an annual summary. At the end of the first year, progress is assessed and operational goals will then be developed for year two, followed by year three.

Connecting Strategic and Operational Goals and Accountabilities

Spreadsheets and tables can become helpful tools to record and define pillars, strategic goals, annual goals, tactics for annual goals, and who will be accountable for implementation. It's helpful to develop an on-screen version of your written strategic plan that can be shared with your governing body and employees. It can then be modified for use with external audiences if desired.

An important note: the twelve-month operating plan is developed by your executive team and leaders in departments associated with the pillars, *not* the board of directors. Unless your organization is run completely by the board of directors with no paid staff (as many small nonprofits are), your governing body should not be driving your firm's operational goals. When the annual operating plan has been completed, your executive team should take it back to the board, council, or trustees and share your annual plan in a follow-up presentation.

Here's an example of how a trade association visually connected strategic goals to annual operating goals, showing how the strategic goals would be measured. This simple slide quickly communicates the linkage between the pillar, the strategic goal, the supporting annual operating goals, and how the strategic goal will be measured.

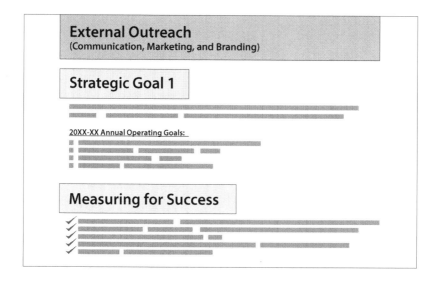

FROM STRATEGIC TO OPERATIONAL: AN AT-A-GLANCE PLAYBOOK FOR SETTING ANNUAL GOALS

After your life-changing workshop that has now created a positive buzz among senior leadership and participants, what happens next? The following week, help your organization fine-tune and finalize the strategic goals. Make sure all of the strategic plan goals supporting the four pillars are crisply stated and are SMART.

Once strategic goals are finalized and approved, the next two to four weeks will be focused on shaping your organization's annual operating goals. Each *strategic* goal will be broken down into one or more enterprise-level *annual* goals to be achieved during the next twelve months. Then, those enterprise-level annual goals will be accomplished by the appropriate work groups and employees.

This is hard work! There's no one right or wrong way to cascade annual goals from the enterprise level to the employee level. Do not aim for perfection. However, *do* aim for clarity and specificity of goal alignment to help your organization determine which business units, departments, divisions, and work groups will support each strategic and annual goal.

I recommend that the process move as quickly as possible following your strategic planning workshop, while momentum is strong. Establish a clear calendar of deadlines for the organization's annual goals, department and division goals, and individual goals monitored at the unit level.

Once the organization's annual goals are approved, each work unit and employee will have more specific goals, such as project- and task-oriented goals that help to accomplish one or more corresponding annual goals. The exact method and length of an organization's annual goal-setting process will vary depending on the size and type of each organization.

Again, it may be comforting to know that there is no one, perfect way to complete the goal cascading process. I recommend that you work with your leadership team to develop an annual goal-setting calendar that works well for your organization's fiscal year.

Encourage each executive and manager to invite input from the employees and work groups responsible for achieving strategic goals. Then, aim for twelve-month SMART goals that clearly state your organization's strategic intent. Strategic intent leads to achieved goals—that is, strategic impact!

For small organizations, such as those with under twenty employees, the core management team may each take a pillar and call staff together to help develop one-year goals. Each goal will be further broken into employee goals and action steps.

For larger organizations, department or division leaders may be asked to collaborate across departments and divisions to shape annual goals pertinent to their unit's responsibilities and deliverables. For further ideas about how to set SMART goals for your annual plan, there are numerous how-to articles available online.

CHAPTER 6

YOUR VITAL TRACKING SYSTEM: SHARED OUTCOMES AND STRATEGIC IMPACT

MOST ORGANIZATIONS GENERATE A PROLIFIC AMOUNT of data—data that can be captured and reported to show strategic plan and annual operating plan goal progress. Goal progress is tangible proof of your organization's *strategic impact*.

Determining exactly what data to capture is key to a meaningful, goal-aligned, effective annual operating dashboard. When leaders communicate results to a board of directors or governing body, it's especially important that the data be easy to interpret as well as to explain.

The third part of any vital strategic plan focuses on tracking progress, communication, and celebrating results. This final part of my equation finishes off a complete and comprehensive strategic planning program. But unfortunately, this is the part that often gets missed!

VITAL STRATEGIC PLANNING =

THE STRATEGIC PLANNING WORKSHOP
(THE SHARED LEADERSHIP EXPERIENCE)

+

THE WRITTEN STRATEGIC PLAN
(THE SHARED STORY OF STRATEGIC INTENT)

+

THE SYSTEM FOR TRACKING
AND COMMUNICATING RESULTS
(THE SHARED GOAL OUTCOMES—THIS IS STRATEGIC IMPACT)

Once your strategic plan is shaped and your organization's strategic and annual operational goals are approved by executive management, it's time to activate your goal-tracking system.

You, as the strategic planning leader for your organization, or the appropriate staff point person, can then put each of the elements—four pillars, corresponding strategic goals, and the annual, twelve-month goals—into a tracking system selected by your organization's executive team to monitor progress.

Building enterprise-level accountability from the division or department level down to the smallest work units is not exactly easy. To do this, many companies are developing strategic plan oversight teams comprised of leaders representing all strategic pillars and an organization's major work departments. These teams typically include all senior executive department heads as well as leaders from human resources and communication departments.

A large hospital's administrative group uses an online tracking system to produce a monthly dashboard for the hospital's monthly board of directors meetings. The dashboard system pulls data from the hospital's electronic medical records. The reports include incidents of patients accidentally falling down while staying at the hospital, prevalence of medical accidents, and other measures.

The red-green-yellow dashboard helps the board focus on red scores—the problem areas—as well as celebrate green scores where hospital staff is exceeding goals. The at-a-glance report simplifies the data and allows board members to ask strategic questions, saving time while enhancing group discussion.

Vital Strategic Plan tracking creates four things: company-wide accountability at the enterprise level; esprit de corps among the entire work force; department or smaller unit accountability; and personal responsibility, when employees clearly see their connection and contribution to their organization's strategic goals. When strategic goals are tracked and progress is documented, reported, and discussed on a regular basis, your strategic plan becomes a credible and powerful tool for driving change and success. It becomes a life changer.

But it's precisely in the *implementation* area where most strategic plans fail—usually because there's no system established for ongoing goal-tracking and discussion.

Due to lack of tracking or the failure to hold managers accountable, coupled with poor communication, 90 percent of organizations fail to execute their strategies successfully.[1]

Based on a study of more than two million employees in 550 companies worldwide, Gallup found that only half of those employees strongly agree that they understand what is expected of them at work. Only 38 percent of managers are engaged in helping employees set priorities.[2] This is a serious problem.

However, the study also found that clarity of employee expectation is connected to as much as a 10 percent *gain* in productivity and 20 percent *fewer* safety incidents.

This is where you can step in and help your executive team review goal-tracking options and agree upon a meaningful, achievable way of gauging results and celebrating successes. This will include determining the individuals who will be responsible for capturing goal performance data. It's important to point out that the greatest tracking system is only as effective as the person or team accountable for monitoring the data and helping the executive team make sense of it.

Even small nonprofit organizations and microbusinesses can track goal progress. As mentioned earlier, the key is to translate strategic planning goals into clearly identified annual goal deliverables with ownership assigned. Keep the annual measurement system as simple as possible.

A nonprofit board chairman turned around a highly distracted, dysfunctional arts organization by using a red-green-yellow quarterly progress report to reduce chatter during meetings. This simple, manually updated dashboard is helping the organization stay on track during board meetings. The dashboard drives discussion about committee assignments, creating focus on accomplishments and next steps.

AN EFFECTIVE TRACKING SYSTEM: IDEAL, BUT NOT PERFECT

Keep in mind that there's no such thing as a *perfect* goal measurement or tracking system. The ideal tracking system will be cost-effective and useful. As part of the vetting process, you and your executive team will review tracking samples to determine the measurement system and dashboard that works best for your organization.

Tracking requires discipline on the part of your organization. Making the connection between annual operating goal progress and three-year strategic goal progress is hard work.

Ongoing goal progress will be reviewed on a consistent basis by each work group and the senior executive team. The status of each annual goal will be assessed. Your color-coded dashboard indicator will help you show how goals are on track (green), in progress (yellow), or where there has been no progress (red).

A visual dashboard or progress report can be generated and shared among work groups and executive management teams for assessment on a monthly, quarterly, semiannual, and annual basis. At the end of each fiscal year, score the progress for each strategic plan goal. You'll connect your organization's twelve-month annual goal achievements to the corresponding three-year strategic goals. Assign someone at the executive level to be accountable for collecting and reporting enterprise-level annual and strategic plan performance data.

When regularly monitored and discussed throughout an organization, an effective tracking system provides high-level visibility of an organization's overall strategy.

EVERY ORGANIZATION NEEDS STRATEGIC PLAN TRACKING

Powerful, cloud-based data collection platforms can make strategic plan tracking easier and more comprehensive than ever in the history of strategic planning.

Online tracking tools can provide a significant relief from the burden of collecting data from numerous departments and producing reports.[3] These typically are subscription-based, online tracking tools using cloud technology to simplify the data collection process. Online tracking tools are especially useful for large- and midsized companies where many departments are accountable for reporting performance metrics.

The number and variety of company performance–tracking dashboard companies is ever growing and changing. Some of the tools are highly customized to fit an organization's nuances, while others feature a more general, off-the-shelf approach.

If the top options for your tracking system are cloud-based, ask for product demonstrations so that your executive team can determine the most effective program. Any subscription-based tracking service should assist your organization with training for those who will be entering goal data.

You can help your organization research the tracking system best suited for the organization's budget and capacity to manage and follow through with reporting. For up-to-the-minute dashboard tools, search the internet for strategic planning dashboards and tracking to find the best solutions for your firm. Budget permitting, these online, cloud-based tracking tools offered by subscription can provide you with a reliable and streamlined reporting system. This includes tracking strategic plan and operational plan goals at all levels of your organization—rolling up data to show unit, department, and enterprise-level progress.

Some companies use more than one tracking dashboard to assess corporate performance.[4] For example:

A corporate strategy performance dashboard can be used to track strategic plans, showing progress for goals, key performance indicators, department data, and underlying factors contributing to corporate performance.

Operational dashboards measure annual goals and day-to-day, month-to-month operational data.

A project portfolio dashboard monitors multiple projects at once, where data for all projects throughout the organization is displayed in one point of reference.

Finally, a benchmarking dashboard compares external and internal benchmark data, placing the needed performance data by the side as benchmarks. Externally, an organization can benchmark competitors to compare performance. Internally, departments can be benchmarked according to performance criteria.

The Fox Chase Cancer Center in Philadelphia, a 2,400-employee healthcare center, was founded in 1904 as one of the nation's first cancer hospitals. It was one of the first centers to earn the comprehensive designation from the National Cancer Institute in 1974 and received the Magnet Designation for Nursing Excellence from the American Nurses Credentialing Center in 2000.

In 2012, after more than a century of operation, the center was purchased by Temple University Health Center. The new strategic planning process included a four-phase cycle including environmental scanning, strategy formulation and validation, strategy implementation and budget planning, strategy evaluation, and performance management.

Following the fourth phase, the organization reevaluated the strategic plan for the next year by returning to phase one, environmental scanning, to assess if new trends and competitive threats required strategy changes for the upcoming year. The strategic planning executive focused on ensuring that every employee from management to frontline staff understood Fox Chase's overall strategies, including how their department was aligning with the strategic plan, and how personal goals for the year contributed to the specific department and center's strategies.

The center's planning department organized educational sessions with department heads and managers to provide strategic plan orientation. This included a quick reference guide.

Fox Chase purchased a ClearPoint Strategy dashboard system. The goal reporting tool was structured to meet the center's specific measurement needs. This included an extensive training program to support those managing the dashboard. The software system was instrumental in helping the center build a culture of performance by automating monthly data analytics and creating visual presentations from the data.[5]

EASY-TO-USE DASHBOARD FOR YOUR ORGANIZATION

Whether your company's tracking tool is a simple spreadsheet with data manually entered, or an online, subscription-based tracking program, use a dashboard to provide an at-a-glance visual to communicate strategic plan goal progress. Assign a point person or multiple trackers across an organization as needed to oversee goal progress reporting.

Strategic plan goal-tracking begins with measuring your organization's progress on twelve-month operational goals that altogether achieve the three-year strategic plan goals. An effective strategic planning tracking report will list each of your company's four pillars. For each pillar, strategic goals will be noted.

Each strategic goal will be supported by one or more annual goals, along with tactics or specific action steps to be completed within your organization's fiscal year. Each annual goal will include how the goal is measured, along with the responsible executive or work group for each goal.

You can create at-a-glance dashboards to visually summarize goal progress. I'm a big fan of color-coded dashboards (usually noted as green, yellow, and red, as mentioned earlier), since these can be used for summary reports to quickly communicate goal progress.

Use Green, Yellow, and Red Colors to Visually Show Progress

For goal progress, use green. For any goal or project stalled or in a holding pattern, use yellow. If no progress has yet been made, use red. (Red or yellow is not always bad; it simply means that progress for certain goals has not occurred *yet*. Often, there are good reasons for delays.)

For Red Scores

Leaders can ask their teams to problem solve. There should be no finger pointing. For example, if you are lagging on sales, invite your team to get to the root of the problem (the "whys"), along with solutions and deadlines.

For Green Scores

Celebrate milestones at company and department staff meetings. Send company-wide e-mails thanking staff for great work. Find ways to celebrate departments, divisions, and employees contributing to goal achievement.

For Yellow Scores

Assess why progress has stalled. If the goal is on hold, determine whether the goal should be removed or updated. Due to rapidly changing market conditions, all goals should be reevaluated midyear and adjusted, or potentially eliminated as market conditions change.

A Simple, Easy-to-Use Dashboard

For small organizations with extremely limited budgets, or for any organization needing to get started with a basic tool for tracking strategic and operational goals, this uncomplicated dashboard can provide a jump-start.

This tracking template connects strategic pillars with strategic goals. Each strategic goal is supported by SMART annual operating goals. Quarterly progress is noted by color-coded circles. Those responsible for each goal are noted in the column to the far right.

PILLAR #	PILLAR DESCRIPTION	HEALTH CENTER EXAMPLE					WHO'S ACCOUNTABLE & COMMENTS
Pillar 1	Programs, Products, & Services	Strategic goal 1. Strengthen the value and assure sustainability of all agency core programs to be offered from 20XX to 20XX.	Q1	Q2	Q3	Q4	Program Director
		By January 30, 20XX, identify agency core programs.	◐	◐	◐	◐	Program Director & CEO
		By March 30, 20XX, ensure every grant funded program has program metrics articulating accountability and data needed to secure and retain grant funding.	O	O	O	O	Program Director
		By March 30, 20XX, ensure every program fits within a packaged theme or family of services.	◐	◐	◐	◐	Program Director
		By Summer 20XX, conduct grand opening of the Center for Men's Health.	●	◐	◐	◐	Program Director
		By Summer 20XX, launch fundraising campaign for the Center for Women's Health.	O	O	O	◐	CEO, Development Director, & Program Director
		By June 30, 20XX, ensure all programs have standard curriculum and that presenters are trained	●	O	O	O	Program Director

◐ = Green O = Yellow ● = Red

At the End of the Fourth Quarter

Use the dashboard to help shape an annual report. Celebrate accomplishments and get ready to begin a new year!

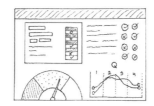

Share and discuss your organization's goal achievements, milestones, and shortfalls at least on a quarterly basis, and preferably on a monthly basis. Use your tracking dashboard tool regularly at board and staff meetings. Use the dashboard at employee one-on-one meetings to facilitate meaningful conversations about individual performance. This will help employees clearly see how their performance contributes to their work unit and organization as a whole.

Each annual operating plan goal should move your organization forward, contributing to the appropriate three-year strategic plan goal. Flexibility is key. If a goal becomes outdated or irrelevant due to changing circumstances, the leadership team can eliminate the goal or revise it as needed. At the end of your organization's fiscal year, be sure to update your strategic plan dashboard if your annual and three-year dashboards are not already connected.

In summary, keep your organization's tracking system or dashboard as simple as possible. Your tracking system should link enterprise-level goals to department goals and individual goals (cascading). Each strategic goal needs to be specific, measurable, and deadline based. Leaders in all departments must follow the same goal-tracking system for consistency. This means they must be trained to effectively share the strategic plan, engage all employees, and track results. This is the most difficult implementation step.

Consider using cloud-based tracking tools if budget permits. Online digital tracking tools are surprisingly cost-effective and efficient in showing vertical (division or department) and horizontal (across department) strategic goal alignment—in other words, how all areas of a company contribute to and impact enterprise-level goals.

Whether your company selects an online tracking system or decides to use a basic spreadsheet, your organization's tracking system should connect strategic goals from the executive or "enterprise" level of your organization to all departments, divisions, or levels of your organization.

––––––––––

CLOUD-BASED STORAGE SYSTEMS

Cloud computing is defined as the on-demand availability of computer system resources, such as data storage, without direct active management by the organization that is using these resources. The term is generally used to describe data centers available to many users over the internet. Computing services are stored and accessed over the internet instead of through physical hard drives. Files and programs stored in the cloud can be accessed anywhere by users, eliminating the need to be near physical hardware, because the data actually lives on a network of hosted servers that transmit data.

Large clouds often have functions distributed over multiple locations from central servers. Clouds can enable organizations to easily track and store data from many company locations, including their strategic planning performance data. Clouds may be limited to a single organization, known as "enterprise clouds," or be available to many organizations, known as a "public cloud." Cloud computing relies on the sharing of resources to achieve coherence and economies of scale.[6]

CHAPTER 7

COMMUNICATE, CELEBRATE, AND ENGAGE EMPLOYEES AND AUDIENCES

STRATEGIC PLANS BECOME POWERFUL, CREDIBLE, AND truly vital when an organization's goals are achieved, communicated, and celebrated. When employees are engaged in their organization's strategic plan and see how their accomplishments contribute to their organization's success, a virtuous circle of future accomplishments is set in motion—that is, a beneficial cycle of goal achievement, each having a reinforcing and positive effect on the next, creating goal momentum in a positive feedback loop.

Companies with engaged employees show higher productivity, better retention, fewer accidents, healthier employees, and 21 percent higher profitability—as much as four times the earnings-per-share for growth than their competitors.[1]

COMMUNICATION AND THE CHANGING WORKPLACE

Workplaces are rapidly changing as technology drives the ability to work differently and stay connected. Effective strategic plan communication can keep employees connected and aligned with the company's direction as well as foster an entrepreneurial mindset, whether employees are centralized, distributed, or home-based. Global corporate culture is changing.

Here are a few trends to consider as you help your company's leadership connect your strategic plan to the ever-evolving, real workplace.[2]

A shift from profit to purpose and values: Help your organization craft clear and crisp vision, mission, and purpose statements that unify employees. Help employees see their interconnectedness to other work groups.

A shift from hierarchical pyramids to a network of teams: Help your organization create a network of talented, multidisciplinary teams that are mission driven and deliver on their strategic plan goals.

A shift from directive leadership to supportive leadership: Your strategic plan can help employees flourish in their work as they are encouraged to focus on team results and less on hierarchy.

A shift from predict-and-plan to experiment-and-adapt: Leaders can encourage experimentation through strategic plan communication. This includes communication that helps employees embrace failure as an important part of the learning process.

A shift from centralized authority to distributed authority: Your company's communication can encourage personal connection to an organization's mission, as well as individual accountability and contribution.

A shift from job descriptions to talents and mastery: Strategic plan communication can provide focus that helps leaders and employees work on priority projects where their interests, talents, and strengths best fit.

A shift from secrecy to radical transparency: When the strategic direction is effectively communicated, leaders boost transparency. This includes talking about and granting access to the strategic plan, strategic and annual operating goals, and ongoing progress reports.

STRATEGIC COMMUNICATION PLAN

As soon as your strategic plan goals are approved and the plan is finalized, work with your executive team and communication staff to create a communication plan to reach both internal and external audiences. Keep your communication plan brief and to the point. Use the communication plan framework to add information about your strategic plan and its key audiences, messages, outreach, and communication activities needed to reach your audiences.

- Ensure all members of executive leadership are personally involved in communicating the strategic plan internally to their employees.

- Appoint a leader to be accountable for external strategic plan communication, promoting goal achievements to constituents when relevant.

- Use digital communication strategies (website, social media, and influencer communication) to reach new and emerging audiences. Experiment with strategic plan key messaging, and refine the message and social media strategies as needed.

Communication Plan Framework

This communication plan framework supports your strategic plan communication. Include the following sections in your plan:

1. Executive summary: a strategic planning summary including brief background about your organization's strategic plan and top-priority goals to support each of the four pillars.

2. Communication goals for supporting and sharing the strategic plan.

3. Your organization's target audiences (internal employees and external publics or stakeholders).

4. Key messages for each target audience.

5. Communication activities (tactics) and a timeline for each strategic plan communication activity, as well as who will be responsible for implementing each tactic. This includes who, within your organization, will be responsible for disseminating information about strategic planning efforts, successes, and tracked results.

6. Timeline for communication.

7. Communication budget.

8. A way to measure, evaluate, and track communication activity, to gauge audience awareness of—and engagement in—your strategic plan.

Questions

Here are some excellent questions to assess the effectiveness of your strategic planning communication efforts:[3]

- Is your leadership team totally aligned with the vision outlined in your organization's strategic plan?

- Have you assessed whether your team understands the strategic plan?

- Do people in the organization understand their roles and responsibilities in achieving the strategic plan?

- Do you have a strategic communication plan in place that sets a rhythm of communication that enforces your objectives, goals, and strategies?

- Is progress on the strategic plan shared with relevant ongoing data to ensure effective execution and decision making to meet timelines?

COMMUNICATION TO SUPPORT YOUR STRATEGIC PLANNING PROCESS

Because strategic planning requires an intense internal focus similar to a special project, I've noticed a tendency for organizations to forget to share progress reports with employees who may not be directly involved in the day-to-day strategic planning activities. Yet there are milestones *during the strategic process itself* that should be shared. Timely, consistent, clear communication is vital for informing and involving employees throughout your organization's strategic planning program or process.

As you work with your strategic planning leadership team, consider creating a tactical communication grid or worksheet to keep your internal audiences in mind and informed during your strategic planning program. The following chart provides a sample of communication activities that require communication to targeted internal audiences.

Note that this sample communication worksheet is separate from your organization's communication plan to support your final strategic plan. You can develop your own worksheet based on your specific strategic plan program activities. For example, if your organization employs fewer than ten people, all employees may be involved in every step.

INTERNAL COMMUNICATION GRID

TYPES OF STRATEGIC PLANNING INFORMATION COMMUNICATED INTERNALLY WITHIN YOUR ORGANIZATION	THE EXECUTIVE TEAM	STRATEGIC PLANNING WORKSHOP PARTICIPANTS	ALL EMPLOYEES
Announcement to kick off the strategic planning process. This includes start and end dates and the end point for completing the strategic plan.	X	X	X
Announcement to share the strategic planning workshop schedule and calendar blockers (date, time, location, pre-meeting homework).	X	X	
Pre-workshop assignment shared: strategic planning executive homework, external focus groups, client and community research, and any assignments to be completed prior to the workshop.	X	X	
Strategic planning workshop agenda for each meeting, including discussion topics.	X	X	
Meeting follow-up notes for each meeting to prepare for future meetings.	X	X	
Draft written strategic plan for executive team review.	X		
Final strategic plan communicated throughout the company, and training or orientation to provide leaders and employees with guidelines for cascading and measuring department and individual goals.	X	X	X
Progress reports shared with management team and entire workforce (ongoing).	X	X	X
Celebrations and executive remarks for strategic goal and milestone achievements (ongoing).	X	X	X

DETERMINE YOUR ORGANIZATION'S BEST INTERNAL COMMUNICATION CHANNELS

Time and time again, research shows that when employees feel aligned with their company's vision, and when they feel informed and listened to, they're much more likely to be engaged and productive. You can help your organization maximize use of internal communication channels, from people as influencers to print and digital publications.

For example, the organization's intranet can serve as a central hub and repository for your strategic plan publications, as well as where you can publish dashboard progress reports. Your intranet can feature strategic plan training materials and supporting documents, such as articles focused on strategic goals.

Consider launching your strategic plan kickoff celebration either in person or virtually at an all-employee meeting. If a large number of your employees work from home or in a distributed environment, an all-employee webinar could be helpful for launching and continuing strategic plan communication.

In virtual meeting settings, some companies use a multipronged communication approach. At a large US company, after an all-employee meeting or call, communication staff are very intentional about follow-up. They leverage diverse internal networks by sending a brief post-meeting survey about the call. Then, staff may personally call up to ten people to discover what employees are talking about, how they feel about the strategic plan and company messaging, and whether a message from a leader had the impact desired. These side conversations help communication leaders keep a pulse on authentic employee feedback and concerns.

IGNITE EMPLOYEE ADVOCACY THROUGH INTERNAL INFLUENCERS

Who are your internal employee influencers? Identify those trusted employee influencers, from entry level to executive ranks, and invite them to help share your key strategic planning messages internally to inspire other employees, as well as externally to their networks.

Create key messages to help these influential employees promote and educate their peers about their organization's strategic plan. Invite your internal influencers to help shape the messaging.[4]

Because your employees know the ins and outs of your brand better than anyone else, encourage them to share their messaging insights with your strategic planning team. Recent research shows that employees want to be involved in co-creating content about their company, and this ownership in the creation process can enhance strategic planning communication.

RECRUIT EMPLOYEES TO BE INFLUENCERS

All employees can get involved in employee advocacy by promoting their company's strategic vision and key strategic goals. Meet as a group or one-on-one to enlist their support for creating their own authentic content combined with strategic plan messaging.

Peer-to-peer communication is a powerful way to create real-life stories about employee innovation, insights, and progress. Feature employee strategic plan success stories and quotes in your company's news channels, e-blasts, intranets, and employee social media pages.

Powerful Storytelling

One of my favorite storytelling models comes from the work of Harvard scholar Marshall Ganz, in telling a public story through his renowned Self-Us-Now model. He includes three elements:

- A story of self: why you were called to do your work.

- A story of us: why your constituency, community, and organization has been called to its shared purposes, goals, and visions.

- And finally, a story of now: the hope to which we can aspire.[*]

Ganz's storytelling model could provide a compelling format for your influencers. You can help them share why they enjoy working at their company (self), why the company is relevant to the world at large (us), and ask them to select their organization's strategic initiative they believe is making a difference (now).

This is a simple but powerful storytelling model. It provides an opportunity for each influencer to authentically connect their story with the company's cause and one or more strategic goals.

This model worked well for a nonprofit organization with a mission of supporting formerly incarcerated women by providing work and life coaching and training after they had served time in the criminal justice system. One of the organization's strategic goals focuses on legislative advocacy for criminal justice reform. The storytelling model helped the organization's clients share their personal story of serving time in jail, how the nonprofit has helped them transform their lives into productive community members, and why criminal justice reform is needed now.

[*] Ganz 2020.

TAKE ON SHORT ATTENTION SPANS
AND INFORMATION CLUTTER

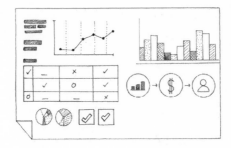

Shorter attention spans, information clutter, people working at multiple locations, and nonstop technology change means that effective communication is more vital than ever before. You have seven seconds or less to grab your audience's attention before you've lost your opportunity. Infographics and visual tools can help bring complex subjects to life through showing more than telling.

Visual tools can help your executive team show how every individual employee, department, and division is aligned to your organization's strategic plan. When connected to your strategic plan, digital animation can help you boost audience engagement, increase information retention, and inform and entertain your audiences. Animated infographics can dramatically bring your strategic plan's static pictures to life. These can include interactive elements, pops of color, or smooth transitions and objects that fade, flash, and move.[5] These subtle microanimations can highlight particular sections in your infographic. This can create a more reader-friendly strategic plan while directing attention to important information.

For example, nonprofit organizations often use infographics to reach donors, volunteers, and many constituents in a cost-effective way, showing how dollars invested resulted in people served, problems solved, and goals reached. That's strategic impact!

Digital animation can provide a low-cost replacement for videos, providing visual assets that can work on all digital platforms including websites, e-blasts, digital newsletters, social media, trade show displays, videos, and traditional printed brochures and mailers. Content can be tailored and targeted to address specific audiences.[6] But remember, you must help your organization create the strategic plan and a tracking system *before* you can produce visual progress reports to monitor and manage your plan.

CELEBRATE STRATEGIC PLAN MILESTONES

When strategic plan goals are achieved, help your executive team create opportunities for employee recognition.

Here are a few celebration ideas:

- Strategic plan major announcements whenever a goal is achieved.

- A thank-you summit with speakers.

- Goal victory rallies.

- Individual, group, and department employee recognition.

- Special project and project leader recognition.

- Company social media celebration.

- A recognition event to bring together board members, senior executives, and staff.

- Employee party at a special venue where family or a guest can be invited.

- Thank-you bonus.

- Extra vacation day as an employee perk.

Fundraising Celebration Creates Momentum

Major fundraising campaigns are similar to strategic plans. Common elements include pre-campaign analysis and homework; setting strategic campaign goals, activities, or tactics leading to donor investments; and ongoing tracking to report results.

Fundraising campaigns can become drawn out and seemingly never-ending, but this was not the case at one university. To add momentum during a multiyear campaign, the university president planned a surprise celebration and dovetailed the rally with a historic donor investment that named a college. It was the largest donor investment ever received by the university.

The university president and college dean drew together the college's faculty, staff, and students, along with community leaders and the media. The celebration included the surprise announcement and introduction to the donor.

Not only did the college naming investment signify a major campaign milestone, it represented the university's fulfillment of a very significant strategic plan goal. The celebration fueled momentum for the remainder of the university's campaign and created community pride.

EXTERNAL COMMUNICATION: PROMOTE YOUR STRATEGIC PLAN TO THE WORLD

In early days of strategic planning, leaders kept these plans tightly held. It was unthinkable to publicly share an organization's strategic goals and aspirations. Today, many global brands publish external versions of their strategic plans as part of their cause-related marketing. Bits of strategic plans can be found on product packaging, websites, and in advertisements. An organization's website is an important, cost-effective global vehicle for communicating the company's mission statement to the world—clearly sharing what it provides, and why.

For example, Uber, the peer-to-peer ridesharing company, uses its website to state its mission, its company values, and a message from the CEO.

Uber's Mission: "We ignite opportunity by setting the world in motion."

Uber introduces the company's story in its "About Us" section, featuring its mission as the headline, followed by two well-crafted sentences to frame its rideshare service: Good things happen when people can move, whether across town or toward their dreams. Opportunities appear, open up, become reality. What started as a way to tap a button to get a ride has led to billions of moments of human connection as people around the world go all kinds of places in all kinds of ways with the help of our technology.

Amazon: "Who we are"

An organization's values help to create connections with customers, supporting brand loyalty. Featured within the "About" section on Amazon's website is a story about the company's guiding values. Amazon is guided by four principles: customer obsession rather than competitor focus, passion for invention, commitment to operational excellence, and long-term thinking. We strive to have a positive impact

---

continued

on customers, employees, small businesses, the economy, and communities. Amazonians are smart, passionate builders with different
backgrounds and goals, who share a common desire to always be
learning and inventing on behalf of our customers.

Similar to Uber and Amazon, your external strategic plan summary
could share your organization's vision, mission, values, and outward-
facing goals to engage and inform your stakeholders and target
audiences. Effective external communication about your strategic plan
can lead to an enhanced brand reputation, including shareholder value.
Your organization can:

- Share strategic plan progress reports with news media. Include
  links to information on your organization's website.

- Post on your organization's social media sites. Encourage internal
  influencers to use key messages and personalize their message,
  using their social media channels.

- Promote strategic plan progress in your annual report, in
  both printed and digital versions, using easy-to-read formats.
  Less is more. Use colorful and interesting infographics to
  convey metrics.

- Publish successes in a variety of internal and external trade
  association and specialty communication venues, including
  social media.

TEN WAYS TO SHOWCASE YOUR ORGANIZATION

Today's digital communication requires strategic messaging and diligent execution. Messages should be brief and focused on inspiring, easy-to-grasp strategic plan imperatives.

Here are ten easy, impactful ways to showcase your organization as an industry leader through authentic, powerful social media techniques. Note that *none* of the following actions require you to compromise confidentiality or competitive advantage.

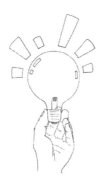

1. Publish a strategic vision report or white paper targeted to your organization's external constituents.

2. Transmit an introduction or cover letter from your organization's CEO or top executive.

    Include important information such as your organization's vision, mission, key initiatives, guiding principles, goals, and board members.

3. Promote your company's thought leadership. Feature a photo or brief video of your team in a planning session, or a guest

speaker who provides industry insight. Show the world how your employees engage with their company's strategic plan.

4. Promote your company's vibrant team. Show photos of your team huddled around flip charts (you can blur confidential, proprietary content on flip charts if needed). This is a great way to promote your team's brilliance.

5. Promote your company's strategic culture. Share a photo of your team having a great time during your planning session. Humanize your company by sharing the team's experience. For example, a work team went bowling after a strategic planning workshop. The leader posted a group photo at the bowling alley with a caption applauding the team's dedication. The post received thousands of views, comments, and likes.

6. Bring in storytellers. Seek the expertise of digital storytellers who can create animated charts and infographics for use on websites and a variety of social media platforms. Engage external constituents such as customers, shareholders, and suppliers, and ask them to share. Measure "clicks" to determine the topics that most people are interested in.

7. Share an important lesson or insight. Share your company's one big lesson learned from the strategic planning experience or share an insight for creating a successful strategic planning session. When you share just one strategic planning tip, you help others learn from your success. For example, was the success of your workshop because of an effective breakout group structure with action-oriented questions?

8. Announce and track one or more of your company's strategic goals publicly. Issue a news release and use social media to boldly proclaim one or more of your top goals for the future. Celebrate and share your tracked success on social media as goals are achieved.

9. Invite input from external influencers. Develop a framework of strategic plan key messages specifically for your influencers. For example, your influencers could personalize and help promote elements of the organization's vision, mission, and one or more strategic goals (e.g., a community impact goal). Carefully select a cadre of credible, visible external influencers to communicate key strategic plan initiatives, such as community leaders and high-profile clients. External influencers can help your company reach new and emerging target audiences. Create opportunities for external influencers to help share your key strategic planning messages on their social media platforms, creating buzz about your company's innovation, insights, and progress.

10. Provide influencer training, sharing key messages, ideas, and communication guidelines. Experiment with strategic plan messages, and refine your influencer outreach program as needed.

MEASURE YOUR STRATEGIC PLAN COMMUNICATION IMPACT

You or someone appointed to follow up strategic plan communication, such as your in-house communication professional, can research and select surveys that measure your communication effectiveness based on the public's *perception* of your organization's value and trustworthiness. The Net Promoter Score (e.g., On a scale of one to ten, how likely are you to recommend our company?) is often a great way to obtain this information.

But remember, this type of ongoing research takes dedicated commitment, expertise, and consistency. Depending on the size of your organization, you may or may not have a department featuring communication and marketing staff with the background needed to be able to gauge and analyze your organization's *communications outcomes*, such as how your organization's strategic plan has impacted internal employee and external audience perceptions. However, you can hire the needed communication research consulting expertise.

There are plenty of communication and digital marketing firms with expertise to help your organization assess your company's strategic plan communication effectiveness, including:

- **Communication plan goals measured** to assess strategic plan employee and public engagement, comprehension, and other key measures.

- **Your social media reach:** the number of people who might have come across your brand (and all relevant content) in social media.

- **Your share of voice:** how much conversation is devoted to your brand, within your niche, industry, product, or service. This indicates popularity.

- **Your sentiment analysis:** how people feel about your brand. This is more subjective and difficult to measure, as certain emotions, such as cynicism, are difficult to detect.

Strategic plan goal-tracking and effective communication about your company's success go hand in hand. By evaluating your firm's communication efforts on a regular basis, your organization is assessing its ability to communicate important strategic planning results—the story of *strategic impact*.

CHAPTER 8

YOUR STRATEGIC PERSONAL PURPOSE: FOR YOU, THE VITAL CURATOR

IT'S BEEN SAID THAT ONLY 1 percent of people across the globe have ever taken the time to contemplate and develop a sense of personal mission or purpose—and that may be overstating it.

This final resource is for you, the strategic planning leader and curator, to be used as a tool to help you discover your *personal* purpose. Your personal purpose statement will serve as a guiding force as you develop your own strategic goals. Your personal purpose statement can provide direction and clarity for all of your career investments, including where and how you choose to work, your volunteer community service, and your lifelong learning efforts.

Your purpose can help you understand what you're passionate about, what you can be best at, and what fuels your internal sense of being, who you are, and what you care about. Moreover, when you more fully understand your own unique sense of purpose (and with it, a compelling leadership pathway), you'll be better equipped to guide, shape, and lead the strategic planning experience for the people and organizations you serve.

The following diagram, which is usually applied to organizations seeking to move from "good" to "great," also can be applied to individual purpose finding. It succinctly illustrates how purpose can direct your life as well as the life of an entire organization.[1]

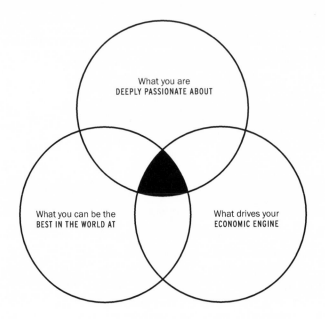

Developed by author and strategy thought leader Jim Collins.

WHY DON'T WE DO IT?

So why do so few human beings ever take the time to consider their personal purpose? Some are afraid of success and the commitment that a personal purpose statement may require. Success requires change, and change alters the relationships around you. While some friends may be supportive, others could be jealous and chide your ambitions.

While the fear of success is often a misunderstood struggle, according to psychologists the fear is likely to have deep roots in a person's past and is based upon the *consequences* of success, not the success itself. For example, rather than move forward to scale up a company, an owner may play small—not at full potential—due to fear of losing friendships and influence with a small, loyal circle of employees.

Shaping a personal purpose is one of several positive ways to face the fear of success head-on and overcome avoidance.

Some people are afraid of failure. If a leader is afraid of failure, it may result in sidestepping plans or conversations about the future. This can include procrastination and overanalyzing the future. The underlying fear of failure is the fear of shame.[2]

The fear of failure can sabotage current goals and future opportunities. To address the fear of failure, the action of shaping a personal purpose can help leaders establish a sense of control and direction in a major area in their lives.

There are many other reasons why people don't take the time to develop a personal purpose. One especially noteworthy reason is that many believe they must have their sense of purpose either perfectly or permanently defined, like a pristine corporate mission statement. But this does not need to be the case.

A personal purpose statement is a work in progress. In fact, it might just consist of a few paragraphs of ideas or a few sentences describing your areas of passion and commitment. It doesn't need to be perfectly wordsmithed.

PERSONAL PURPOSE PERSONAL REFLECTION

1. Answer the following questions:

- How would you like to be remembered many years from now by those who knew you?

_____

_____

_____

_____

- What would you do *now* if there were no risk of failing?

  _____

  _____

  _____

  _____

  _____

- What are two times in recent years where you felt as if you were making a difference? Describe them in as much detail as you like.

  _____

  _____

  _____

  _____

  _____

- How can you immediately ensure you live your purpose each day with no regrets? Examples include not living your life to please others, or expanding personal learning outside of your day-to-day work.

  _____

  _____

  _____

  _____

  _____

- What is the purpose of my life? I believe the purpose of my life is to (describe or write in as much detail as you choose):

  _____

  _____

  _____

  _____

  _____

- When will you find time to reflect on your purpose? (Describe when you'll take time to think deeply about your personal purpose and assess opportunities to align your work, career, and personal life.)[3]

_____

_____

_____

_____

_____

2. Observe themes or patterns.

- Do you see or sense apparent themes or patterns? Themes could include wanting to make a difference through artistic skills and creativity, wanting to make an impact in equality and social justice in one's community, or using your teaching skills to make a difference in business settings.

   Observe themes or patterns that reveal the *unique and real you*. Summarize those in paragraphs, bullets, or just descriptive words. Don't worry about being precise! Just get your ideas on paper and reflect on and refine them over time. Your personal purpose is a process, and it will *continue to evolve*.

_____

_____

_____

_____

3. Assess your career investments.

Take stock of your existing professional, volunteer, and lifelong learning investments. Ensure that your career, volunteer service, and lifelong learning investments are aligned with and support your purpose.

4. Use these personal purpose resources.

- Mission and purpose statement examples:
  https://www.missionstatements.com.

- Executive mission and purpose statement examples: https://
  www.fastcompany.com/3026791/personal-mission-statements-
  of-5-famous-ceos-and-why-you-should-write-one-too.

- The Five-Step Plan for Creating Personal Mission Statements.[4]

5. Stay inspired.

Here are a few inspirational leaderships quotes I truly hope
will spark your unique personal purpose and strategic planning
genius.

There are no superheroes, just us.
We are the ones we've been waiting for.

—Shiza Shahid, Malala Fund Co-Founder, 2013

The biggest risk is not taking any risk. In a world
that is changing really quickly, the only strategy that
is guaranteed to fail is not taking risks.

—Mark Zuckerberg, 2011

We desperately need more leaders who
are committed to courageous, wholehearted
leadership and who are self-aware enough to lead
from their hearts, rather than unevolved leaders
who lead from hurt and fear.

—Brené Brown, 2018

We delight in the beauty of the butterfly,
but rarely admit the changes it has gone
through to achieve that beauty.

—Maya Angelou

CONCLUSION

CLOSING THOUGHTS

AS I STATED FROM THE BEGINNING, you are a *life changer*! Strategic planning is difficult, vital work.

From the moment you start planning the workshop, you are creating a shared experience. You're inspiring meaningful conversations and making a place for historic moments in time in the life of an organization. You are helping leaders get beyond company silos so that they can vocalize their hopes, dreams, ideas, and strategic vision.

This book presents a meaningful, flexible three-part formula to help you work with your organization's executive team and shape a vital strategic planning program. While it delivers a time-tested approach with a framework for each part of the formula, the Vital Strategic Plan is never boilerplate, nor is it simplistic. However, this easy-to-use framework allows even the smallest organizations to create a vital strategic planning program, adapting the framework as needed.

The Vital Strategic Plan is a shared human leadership experience. While your strategic plan will produce growth for your organization, the strategic planning *experience* will produce personal growth for those who participate. The experience will ultimately create ownership of the plan—ownership that will drive commitment to results.

VITAL STRATEGIC PLANNING =

THE STRATEGIC PLANNING WORKSHOP
(THE SHARED LEADERSHIP EXPERIENCE)

+

THE WRITTEN STRATEGIC PLAN
(THE SHARED STORY OF STRATEGIC INTENT)

+

THE SYSTEM FOR TRACKING
AND COMMUNICATING RESULTS
(THE SHARED GOAL OUTCOMES—THIS IS STRATEGIC IMPACT)

In addition to what you have discovered in this book, the appendix contains more of my favorite and most vital strategic planning consulting tools, techniques, activities, and tips from which you can choose. Don't forget that you can conduct some or all of your strategic planning program virtually, if in-person workshops are not an option for the particular dynamics of your organization.

You can and should modify all of the workshop, written plan, tracking, and communication tools I have presented throughout this book to fit your organization's needs. Or, you can develop your own tools.

I wish you the thrill of strategic planning as you inspire leaders and their organizations.

ACKNOWLEDGMENTS

STRATEGIC IMPACT: A LEADER'S THREE-STEP FRAMEWORK for the Customized Vital Strategic Plan is the result of an incredibly gifted team of wise advisors and collaborators.

I am indebted to my clients and colleagues in every organization where I've served during the past three decades—either as an employed leader or as a strategic planning consultant. Each firm's unique challenges shaped my strategic planning insight and helped me develop the Vital Strategic Plan framework. From years of practice, I learned to put a premium on cultivating meaningful leadership experiences and strategy-shaping workshops resulting in plans that get communicated and implemented.

I thank the strategy thought leaders and scholars whose important work has contributed to my practice and is referenced throughout this book.

I'm grateful for my exceptional publisher team, Fast Company Press and Greenleaf Book Group. As a steadfast subscriber to *Fast Company* magazine since its inception, I knew this publishing partnership was destined to be. The publishers believed in my innovative strategic planning approach. They applauded my courage to create a new strategic planning model and to incorporate digital strategies not available until now. They shared enthusiasm for my chapter about virtual strategic planning that was added as our world faced the COVID-19 global pandemic.

I'm blessed to have worked with Sally Garland, whose talent for business storytelling challenged me to spotlight some of my how-to tools and techniques, as well as add more case studies to make the book more useful. I'm grateful for copy editor Anne Sanow, who ensured pristine crispness for the final manuscript. These expert editors are world-class.

I greatly appreciate Chase Quarterman's contemporary design, putting hours of care into the various sections, sidebars, and worksheets to create user-friendly readability and gravitas.

I thank my team of Greenleaf Book Group mentors for sharing their business and marketing wisdom, including Justin Branch, Sam Alexander, Jen Glynn, Tiffany Barrientos, O'Licia Parker-Smith, and Emily Maulding.

I truly am fortunate that my son, animator and creative director Justin Poore, created brilliant illustrations that breathed life into strategic planning as a vital leadership experience.

Finally, as a former nonprofit CEO who helped a healthcare organization navigate tough times, I am deeply thankful for executive teams who are leading organizations around the world with little to no strategic planning budget. In moments when I was immersed in a dense fog of research, synthesizing, and writing, I remembered you, my reader. I envisioned how this book would become a comprehensive guide for your organization's Vital Strategic Plan. The very thought of you kept me inspired with purpose.

VITAL STRATEGIC PLANNING TOOLS, TEMPLATES, AND TECHNIQUES

IN THIS APPENDIX YOU WILL FIND a variety of helpful tools, templates, and techniques for custom designing your organization's strategic planning program, including further explanation of several tools already discussed in this book. Use them as "plug and play" resources to insert into your strategic planning workshop agenda.

These effective tools, templates, and techniques—plus others you may discover, embellish, or invent for your organization—will help you create a *customized* vital strategic planning program.

Leadership Map

My Leadership Map is one of my favorite go-to tools to quickly and visually show the linkage between an organization's vision, mission, strategic pillars for success, strategic goals, and annual (twelve-month) operating goals. The map shows how each piece of the strategic framework is interconnected.

This diagram provides a big-picture overview tool. This is *not* a goal-tracking template.

As your strategic planning team shapes strategic goals during the workshop, you can fill in each section of this template. This slide can be presented at the beginning of your workshop, showing the map's blank areas to be discussed and completed. As each element is completed, this slide can be updated and shared at intervals throughout your workshop.

You can include this visual in your written strategic plan. It also could be used as an interactive digital infographic with each component featuring links to supporting information. Over time, you can continue to revisit the map as your team provides strategic plan updates.

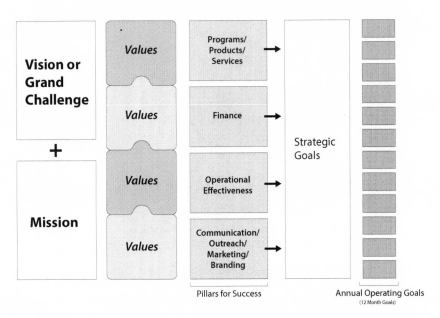

Leadership Map © Carol A. Poore.

Living Timeline

The living timeline is one of my favorite welcome activities to kick off a strategic planning workshop. The living timeline is a large paper timeline featuring your company's history and major milestones. Participants will be treated to a very powerful and unifying leadership experience if you utilize this during your opening events and welcome activities. I've found that when you use the timeline with the intent of creating inclusion and a safe space to share from the heart, it is a brilliant warm-up tool for quickly creating a spirit of teamwork and bonding. The inclusion it fosters comes through the use of brief storytelling sessions.

The activity shows the group why each person in attendance is a vital part of the organization. Don't be surprised if you see some tears flow and hugs being shared. This timeline provides an opportunity to honor the past while preparing for the future.

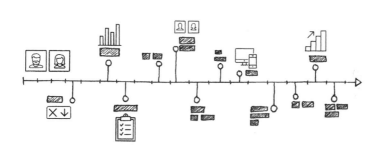

How to Create a Living Timeline

1. Purchase a roll of butcher paper. It is available at most office supply stores.

   - Start by writing in major milestones dating from the organization's founding date through the present. Add a future date three years into the future or further if you wish.

   - Include photos, illustrations, and brief descriptions.

   - Your timeline can be simple and handwritten, or it can be elaborately designed with computer-generated text and graphics based on your organization's budget, time, staff support, and culture.

   - Place your timeline on a large wall in the room where your group will gather for one of your opening activities.

2. Begin the timeline event with the facilitator or organization's top leader providing a high-level history of the organization's major accomplishments as they point to each of the individual company

continued

milestones noted on the timeline. This should take no more than 10 minutes.

3. Following a brief company overview, the facilitator or leader will invite each person to come up to the timeline. One by one, and taking approximately 2 to 3 minutes, each person will be asked to share:

- When he or she joined the organization.

- Why he or she joined the organization.

- If appropriate, any brief personal milestones that brought them to the organization or to the workshop.

- Why they're proud to serve the organization at the present time.

- One unique claim to fame, mastermind skill, or personal celebrity gift that they have to contribute to the company's success.

- Why they're excited about the organization's future.

4. After each employee shares his or her brief story, each person will initial the timeline with a marker, placing initials at the year (or time era) when he or she joined the organization.

Tracking Tools for Tracking Goals

Online goal measurement is a rapidly growing, evolving industry. A number of cloud-based strategic plan online tracking programs are available to you today on a subscription basis. I recommend that you research options for your organization's online goal-tracking system. You can request a demonstration to see firsthand how these tools could be applied to your organization's strategic planning program. Your executive team will make the final decision based on cost, tracking features, training opportunities for staff who will use the tracking system, and other criteria.

Companies such as ClearPoint Strategy track company-wide goal progress in an efficient, cost-effective, and visually impressive way. If your organization has multiple businesses and hundreds of employees, a simple Excel spreadsheet is not going to be the most efficient way to keep track of your strategic plan, due to the multiple inputs needed for large-scale tracking. These cloud-based tracking tools provide customizable software that measures your goals, and they allow your organization to personalize the tools with your official logo and colors to provide a customized, branded look.

Benefits of Cloud-Based, Online Tracking Systems

- They connect all goal-related operational (twelve-month) goals and related activities across your company's divisions, departments, and work units.

- Strategic plan goals can be revised or eliminated as needed.

- Goal accountability or ownership can be assigned, collaborators noted, and goals, tactics, timeliness, and results can be linked.

- Administrator and individual user access can be controlled with user password protection.

- Tracking software sends automated reminders when projects and goal deliverables are due. These gentle reminders save hours of managerial time.

- Software generates summaries for strategic planning executives and the board of directors that can be exported into on-screen presentations and written reports.

- If your organization lacks the sufficient budget to subscribe to an online tracking system, it still can benefit from a manual spreadsheet system, at least to get started. Your executive team will want to appoint a person or team to be accountable for your organization's strategic plan tracking. All departments contributing data should use the same spreadsheet format to enable data to be easily imported into the master report.

Internal Analysis: SWOT Analysis Chart

SWOT analysis provides an excellent executive pre-workshop homework assignment. While some strategic planners critique SWOT as an outdated method, many have developed modifications of this thought process. I believe that SWOT still is an extremely valuable analytical tool, in combination with other internal analysis techniques such as Fail-Succeed and appreciative inquiry.

The SWOT worksheet template can be shared on-screen during your strategic planning workshop. Spend the most time assessing your organization's strengths and opportunities. Explore how your organization's strengths create unique competitive advantage.

During your workshop, share a very succinct version of your SWOT findings on-screen, so that everyone can clearly see it. You also could provide a copy for each participant's packet. To keep the discussion focused on the most critical findings, I recommend presenting the most important observations from each SWOT category rather than reading all items.

	STRENGTHS	WEAKNESSES
I N T E R N A L	• LIST IN BULLETS... SUCCINCT DESCRIPTIONS • LIST IN BULLETS... SUCCINCT DESCRIPTIONS • ETC...	• LIST IN BULLETS... SUCCINCT DESCRIPTIONS • LIST IN BULLETS... SUCCINCT DESCRIPTIONS • ETC...
	OPPORTUNITIES	THREATS
E X T E R N A L	• LIST IN BULLETS... SUCCINCT DESCRIPTIONS • LIST IN BULLETS... SUCCINCT DESCRIPTIONS • ETC...	• LIST IN BULLETS... SUCCINCT DESCRIPTIONS • LIST IN BULLETS... SUCCINCT DESCRIPTIONS • ETC...

A Simple Strategic Plan Goal-Tracking Template

This easy-to-create template is an example of a simple, cost-effective goal-monitoring tool requiring manual input and no subscription. Your dashboard can be created in a spreadsheet. Scores (red, green, or yellow) are manually added each quarter. List each strategic pillar theme to the far left. List the strategic goal, followed by the twelve-month operational goals. Report progress on each goal at the end of every quarter. Red signifies that no progress has been made yet. Yellow indicates that the goal is in progress, or that some progress has been made. Green notes that the goal has been accomplished.

Pillar 1: Programs, Products, and Services

Goal theme	Lead	FYXX Goals	How measured				
Programs, Products, and Services		Goal 1: List strategic goal (List Year) Annual Operating Goal(s):	Quarterly Progress	Q1 ◉	Q2 ○	Q3 ○	Q4 ○
Programs, Products, and Services		Goal 2: List strategic goal (List Year) Annual Operating Goal(s):	Quarterly Progress	Q1 ●	Q2 ○	Q3 ○	Q4 ○
Programs, Products, and Services		Goal 3: List strategic goal (List Year) Annual Operating Goal(s):	Quarterly Progress	Q1 **O**	Q2 ○	Q3 ○	Q4 ○
Programs, Products, and Services		Goal 4: List strategic goal (List Year) Annual Operating Goal(s):	Quarterly Progress	Q1 **O**	Q2 ○	Q3 ○	Q4 ○

◉ = Green O = Yellow ● = Red

A Communication Plan Template
to Support Your Strategic Plan

Keep your communication plan brief and to the point. Include the following sections in your plan.

1. Executive summary: a strategic planning summary including key goals and brief background about your organization's strategic plan.

2. Communication goals for supporting and sharing the strategic plan.

3. Your organization's target audiences (internal employees and external publics or stakeholders).

4. Key messages for each target audience.

5. Communication activities (tactics) and a timeline for each strategic plan communication activity, as well as who will be responsible for implanting each tactic. This includes who, within your organization, will be responsible for disseminating information about strategic planning efforts, successes, and tracked results.

6. Timeline for communication.

7. Communication budget.

8. A way to measure, evaluate, and track communication activity, to gauge audience awareness of—and engagement in—your strategic plan.

Communication Plan Worksheet at-a-Glance Grid

Here's a communication plan at-a-glance template featuring an action plan to support your strategic planning program. Use this as a supplementary document to accompany your communication plan. It's an excellent tool for planning and documenting communication activities, clearly showing how promotion tactics advance your organization's strategic plan communication opportunities.

continued

STRATEGIC PLAN COMMUNICATION OPPORTUNITY		COMMUNICATION GOAL	COMMUNICATION STRATEGY AND TACTICS			COMMUNICATION MEASUREMENTS
Describe Opportunity	Audience	Expected Outcomes	Key Message(s)	Media/ Timing	Cost	How Evaluated

Opening Activities: Shared Experiences and Magical Moments

When your meeting begins, it's crucial to make sure that all participants introduce themselves with a simple storytelling moment. This pleasantry is often forgotten in the hurry to conquer the agenda. In virtual settings, informal discussion prior to the meeting start time is even more important, bringing the power of human connectivity to your meeting. Traditional meeting icebreakers can eat up precious time and feel forced, and the term "icebreaker" is often perceived as a forced, boring activity.

From the moment people arrive, all of your activities should help you build progress toward the purpose of your meeting. If people know each other well, select a group introduction that adds an element of surprise or leadership learning.

While these brief exercises can be fun, many are not designed as collective group bonding experiences. Aim to create a new level of shared experience through a very brief personal storytelling experience.

Introductions: Brown Paper Bag + Personal Item

This exercise is one of my favorites. It's an easy, no-risk way to quickly create deeper human connections among participants because each individual gets to choose what he or she will share. With your meeting invitation, provide a small, plain brown paper bag. Ask your participants to find a small object at home that connects to something they like to do or connects to a significant event in their lifetime. This could be a trophy, a photo, a toy. The possibilities are endless. This object can be held up and shared on-screen, if your meeting is virtual.

During opening introductions, ask each participant to share, in a minute or less, what the object is, why it was and still is important, and how the object continues to impact his or her future. Participants will learn something new about each person in the room. These moments make for the life-changing experience you want to provide.

Introduce Your Colleague

The facilitator asks all participants to write down three questions and find someone in the room they do not know well. The questions could be simple, such as asking where participants are from or sharing a favorite hobby. Or, share your greatest work-related accomplishment so far in your career.

Another option is to have participants turn to the person sitting next to them for this conversation. Then the facilitator asks participants to introduce their conversation partners to the group by sharing both the questions and recapping the answers. This activity encourages listening, and fosters team discovery and appreciation.

A variation of this activity can have the facilitator presenting two or three questions that fit the theme for the strategic planning session. These might ask participants to describe one skill they are proud of that makes a difference in the organization's success, or to describe a life experience that has helped them to become a stronger person.

Appreciative Inquiry

Appreciative inquiry (AI) is a strengths-based model that seeks to engage stakeholders in self-determined change. AI distinguishes itself from other organizational visioning and change models by focusing on "the best of what is," and using this as a platform to build group directions.

AI principles can be incorporated into pre-workshop activities such as employee or customer focus groups. AI could be used to follow a SWOT analysis. The AI process includes four distinct phases, called the 4D Cycle.

- *Discovery:* participants explore the best of what is, identifying the organization's strengths, best practices, and sources of excellence, vitality, and peak performance.

- *Dream:* participants envision a future they really want—a future where the organization is fully engaged and successful around its core purpose and strategic objectives.

- *Design:* participants leverage the best of what is and their visions for the future to design high-impact strategies that move the organization creatively and decisively in the right direction.

- *Destiny (sometimes also called Deploy):* participants put the strategies into action, revising as necessary.

More Facilitation Techniques

It takes years of practice for facilitators to think on their feet during difficult situations, including how to handle conflict in a constructive way and how to create contingency plans when circumstances change, such as a valuable conversation requiring more than the allotted time. Because no two meetings are alike, even the most experienced facilitator may occasionally be caught off guard with an unanticipated disruption.

Here are two situations that create potential strategic planning distraction: when executives signal they are bored or too busy, and when heated arguments occur where agreement cannot be reached.

Tips for Facilitating Busy Executives

Facilitation includes listening and improvising. Listening means not only paraphrasing what people are saying to confirm your understanding, but being capable also of reading the room. As you or your facilitator presents, watch the reactions of the audience. Be willing to address what you observe happening, and if necessary, alter the agenda and improvise if needed.* The following techniques should be employed if people seem bored, disengaged, engage in side talk, or leave the room.

- **Use a time cut** and be prepared with a shorter, five-minute version of the workshop activity.

---

continued

- **Reconfirm why the topic is still important** if people start checking their e-mail or looking at their watches or phones. Request help from your sponsor or the most senior person.

- **Stop the person who is leaving** and ask what to do next, such as wait until she returns or move forward with the decision.

- **Improvise** by changing the topic or direction.

- **Capture what is being said in an alternative discussion** and then reconfirm at the end of the discussion.

When No Agreement Can Be Reached, Try the Following

- Propose a break, silent thinking time, or postponing the decision to a later date to give people time to cool down and reflect. If the decision is postponed, it is often a good idea to engage conflicting parties in conflict resolution before the issue is brought up again.

- Ask those disagreeing for alternative proposals.

- Agree on a process for making a decision that all parties can sign on to. When one or two people are blocking consensus and won't budge, ask if they are prepared to stand aside and allow the group to proceed with the action. It may help if the group assures them that the lack of unity will be recorded in the minutes, that the decision does not set a precedent, and that they won't be expected to implement the decision.

- Negotiate with holdouts and ask: What would it take to get you on board with this strategy or idea? You could ask: Are there any points on which you agree and can move forward? How important is the exact wording for this strategy now? Is there a group who can take the idea offline and refine the wording?

- Don't mistake silence for consent—encourage a response from every participant.

> - The group should be conscious of making a contract with each other. If an agreement is reached too easily, then check to make sure that members really are fully supportive of the decision and do agree on essential points.[†]
>
> [*] Gilbert 2019.
> [†] Seeds for Change 2019.

HeartMath

HeartMath (https://www.heartmath.com/about) was founded in 1991 by Doc Childre, who developed scientifically based tools and technologies to bridge the intuitive connection between heart and mind and deepen connection with the hearts of others. Based on the training and exercises on the website, an opening group exercise or group activity could be offered after breaks.

Meeting in a Box

You can easily create what is a great technique for community planning and for providing community leaders with facilitated presentations and discussion guides that cover critical topics. An organizing group, such as a community downtown organization, may be accountable for creating content and distributing the meeting information to other groups, such as neighborhood groups.

The organization group will be responsible for creating the meeting materials, and assembling and delivering the meeting boxes to participating group leaders. Include a facilitator guide, handouts, meeting ideas, and breakout exercises. A cost-effective plus: files can be provided on a USB, with master hard copy in each box.

One-Word Opening and Closeout

A simple technique to create a participative and authentic start and ending to any meeting—that works well for both in-person and virtual meetings—is the one-word opening and closing. Ask participants to share one word, and one word only, to describe how each person is feeling about a topic. It could be about the organization, or a particular strategy, or the strategic planning experience itself. This technique helps participants express themselves succinctly, and it creates a tone of authenticity and focus.

1-2-4-All

1-2-4-All, created by Liberating Structures, is an exercise that engages everyone simultaneously in generating questions, ideas, and suggestions. Participants own their ideas, requiring at least 12 minutes of total time. The five structural elements creating the structure include developing the conversation invitation, arranging the conversation, proper space and materials, determining levels of participation, and deciding how groups will be configured, followed by the four steps measured in minutes.[1]

The Basic Steps for 1-2-4-All

1. Ask a question in response to the presentation of an issue, or about a problem to resolve or a proposal put forward, such as: What opportunities do you see for making progress on this challenge? How would you handle this situation? What ideas or actions do you recommend?

2. For the one question you ask, break activities into the following time segments:

- **The first minute:** silent self-reflection by individuals on a shared challenge, framed as a question (e.g., What opportunities do *you* see for making progress on this challenge? How would you handle this situation? What ideas or actions do you recommend?).

- **The next two minutes:** generate ideas in pairs, building on ideas from self-reflection.

- **The next four minutes:** share and develop ideas from your pair in foursomes (notice similarities and differences).

- **The final five minutes:** return to the plenary group. Ask: What is one idea that stood out in your conversation? Each group shares one important idea with all.

This cycle could be repeated as needed to address additional topics. Supporters of this exercise note the efficiency of time without taking a political approach. Critics argue that when the group jumps to "all," asking groups to throw away other ideas limits creative thinking and sacrifices other important perspectives.

This exercise could be augmented by asking that smaller groups bring back three top ideas. More time could be allotted to the final plenary session, such as 15 minutes instead of five minutes.

Think Big

As an add-on to any assignment, each homework team could be asked to think big: think about what is *possible* for your organization's growth and development. Based on your competitive intelligence investigation, what does your company need to do to grow, thrive, and achieve new possibilities?

Gap Analysis

This is an excellent executive homework assignment. Create your own diagram in a homework sheet to help your teams review and analyze where your organization is now, and where it needs to be. Note any existing gaps.

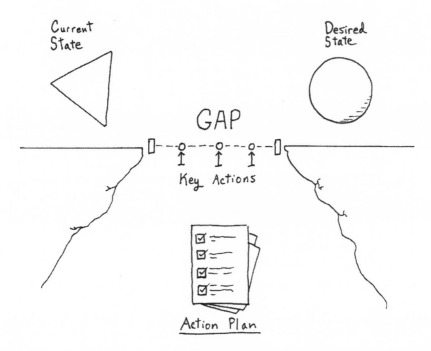

Ground Rules

Ground rules are important for keeping your organization's strategic planning participants focused, supportive, productive, and on track. The facilitator asks the leadership team to share these rules with workshop participants so that the group guidelines are set and communicated up front. That way, participants can hold themselves accountable for living by their norms. Ground rules apply to both in-person and virtual strategic planning meetings.

Ground Rule Examples

1. Everyone is expected to:

   - Arrive to the meeting a few minutes prior to start time.

   - Arrive back to the meeting on time following scheduled breaks.

   - Stay for the entire workshop. This shows respect and commitment to the process, and to the organization's future.

2. No cell phone calls or texting until scheduled breaks.

3. Brainstorming and input sessions are not to be critically judged. All ideas are welcome! Ideas will be summarized and further vetted. Everyone is expected to:

   - Respectfully listen to others with full attention and no judgment.

   - Respect individual confidentiality as well as proprietary company information being discussed.

   - No side conversations or criticism for others' opinions.

   - Everyone is encouraged to express his or her viewpoints. Disagreements will be shared with respect, not criticism.

   - Use of a "parking lot" flip chart will record important issues not relevant to the current discussion.

   - One person speaks at a time and will be acknowledged by the facilitator.

   - People who miss a meeting or part of a meeting have the responsibility to catch up by contacting someone who attended.

4. For virtual meetings, the "lights-camera-action" ground rule is both important and easy to remember. There should be plenty of light on each participant's face so that all participants can be seen on everyone's screens. The camera should provide a close-up view of each participant for eye-to-eye contact. There should be no distracting action or activity in the background to detract from the virtual meeting.

Meeting Dynamics: Plan for Plan B

Plan for the unexpected. You—the curator, leader, or facilitator—have to be able to think fast and reroute activities during your strategic planning workshop if circumstances arise that demand a change of course. Consider back-up plans for any unexpected "what-if" meeting contingencies.

Anticipate which activities could be moved, abbreviated, added, or cut out altogether to streamline the workshop. You can always choose to end the day earlier than scheduled. (Your participants will love receiving the gift of time.)

Common Plan B Situations

UNEXPECTED MEETING SITUATIONS	CONTINGENCY IDEAS FOR PLAN B
Your opening panel or expert guest speaker fails to show, plane delayed, etc.	Use a virtual meeting tool such as Zoom, Webex, Google Hangouts, or other technology to create an opportunity for the speaker to virtually attend.
	Tap a different expert speaker and, if from out of town, bring into the meeting using technology.
	Create a surprise panel from the attendee list and ask them to assist with the same or a different topic.
	Open your strategic planning program with a great video from a recent keynote or prominent speaker.
	Skip the speaker and ask the audience to be the topic experts. Give audience members a three-minute limit to share what they know about your opening strategic issue.
An important discussion or exercise goes 20 minutes too long. The strategic planning workshop now is behind schedule.	Shorten the scheduled breaks.
	Abbreviate one or more upcoming agenda activities.
	Eliminate or postpone an activity. Or, assign breakout groups to parse out and accomplish an activity within a compressed time allotment. Ask each breakout team to share results with the entire group.

You discover that the workshop needs to be pulled together in a more clear and compelling way at the end due to the many issues discussed.	During one of the breaks, develop a few closing slides to emphasize what was prioritized and next steps.
AV failure, power outage, etc. impacting your on-screen presentation.	Provide hard-copy handouts and share the presentation verbally. Skip to another exercise and return to the presentation when the issue is resolved. Make sure all speakers bring back-up notes, and have speakers continue the presentation.

Fail-Succeed Goal-Setting

This technique forces executives to recognize worst-case scenarios by first asking: What would it take to fail? The Fail-Succeed exercise forces participants to take off their rose-colored glasses and critically examine each major pillar of their organization. You will first divide participants into four pillar breakout groups (Programs, Products, and Services; Financial; Operational Effectiveness; and External Outreach). During this part of the exercise, a selected group facilitator will ask each group to indicate what it would take to *fail* in each of the assigned pillars, being as specific as possible. For external outreach, for example, failure points might include the failure to update an organization's website, or failure to produce timely news and information about the organization in a digital world where everyone expects instant communication.

- Each breakout group should describe the failure point in detail. This will allow the group to later pinpoint a very specific solution for turning the potential failure into a strategic success. For example, the financial breakout team would discuss every possible way the organization might experience financial failure and record them in specific detail on flip charts posted on one or more large wall spaces. Instead of saying "lack of revenue," the failure point should be described in vivid detail such as "revenue declines because XYZ product or service becomes obsolete."

- The breakout group facilitators will continue to probe the what-it-would-take-to-fail issues until each group has exhausted all possible answers. When there are no more failure ideas being vetted, each of the breakout groups will rotate, in a Round-Robin activity, to all other breakout areas, contributing additional failure points on the flip charts if they believe key points are missing.

- Each breakout team will rotate clockwise to all of the breakout rooms, spending five minutes or so in each room. You, the facilitator, will direct the groups when it's time to continue rotating. Once participants have added any missing failure points to all of the pillar rooms, they will rotate back to the home-base room.

- Next, for each failure point, each pillar team will create a very specific success strategy. It's important to note that the success strategy should not simply state the opposite of each failure point. Each success strategy should be SMART, and it should counter the failure point. By being as specific as possible about the success strategies to overcome failure points, each pillar group is already in the process of drafting SMART goals for each of the pillars.

SMART Goal Definition: Specific, Measurable, Achievable, Realistic, and Time-Based

Once strategic goals have been brainstormed, you or the facilitator will ask your entire executive team to move around the four pillar breakout areas and vote with sticky dots on priority goals. Voting allows these goals to quickly and clearly rise to the top in a very democratic, visible manner.

The labor of shaping strategic goals for each of the pillars is the hardest part. While the Fail-Succeed exercise is profoundly effective and quick, the Succeed part of this exercise requires participants to create specific solutions to overcome failure points. Then, those success recommendations will require even further work—usually offline, away from the strategic planning workshop—to make even more specific and measurable. Once strategic goals are shaped and prioritized, the executive team will determine the *operational goals*—what needs to be accomplished in the twelve months ahead.

Voting with Sticky Dots

When strategies have been shaped, voting with sticky dots can provide a fast, participative indication of board and executive team priorities. This is not a scientific survey, nor is it a thumbs-up/thumbs-down or pass/fail exercise. This simple step provides a fast way to quickly assess top priorities based on the knowledge and concerns of those participating in your strategic planning workshop. The sticky dot voting exercise has been used for decades. It engages participants in opinion sharing, gets them moving around, and can be fun.

For virtual strategic planning, there are online voting and polling apps that resemble in-person sticky dot exercises. For example, GroupMind is a collective intelligence software for virtual idea generation, voting, and discussion. PollUnit uses round virtual dots for online opinion sharing. For in-person strategic planning, participants are each given a number of colored sticky dots and are asked to vote on recommended strategies for each of an organization's strategic pillars. They place the dot stickers next to the strategies they believe are top priority or most critical to the success of the organization's future. It's helpful to limit the number of dots to three votes to be spent on any one initiative, so that no one can game the system and put all of their dots on one item. After the voting, the priorities will be clearly seen by the entire group. This exercise provides a very democratic and visible way to prioritize strategic goals.

Plenary Session Recap: Share Only the Top-Priority Insights

After a strategic goal (Fail-Succeed) discussion culminating in a voting exercise, it's important to bring the results back to the entire (plenary) group of participants. This provides a robust way to recap the most vital insights and strategies, and also provides closure to the most important part of the strategic planning workshop.

After your Fail-Succeed and voting exercise, ask participants to bring their top picks for the highest-ranking priority strategies selected. Ask each team to *limit the priorities* to the top three or top five to save time and to provide large-group focus on the most important strategic goals. You don't need to do any wordsmithing. Staff can refine the wording later for the priority goals and determine other success strategies that should be included.

Parking Lot

Keep one or two blank flip charts posted in your main meeting room labeled "parking lot." When participants ask off-topic questions or bring up topics not pertinent to your discussion, acknowledge the topic and recommend that the topic be added to the parking lot so that it can be addressed at the end of the day or at a follow-up meeting. This technique recognizes input and important topics while keeping your group focused and on point.

Strategic Options, Happy Stories

This pre-workshop exercise is imaginative and helps leaders visualize a vibrant, successful future. The assignment should focus on the entire organization and its future horizon—its future state. The team can later work backward to determine what would need to happen for this happy future to become a reality, using the Fail-Succeed technique to determine strategic goals.

Strategic options can be described as a happy story about the future. It doesn't have to be right, and it doesn't even have to be sensible. It must result in your organization being in a happy place in the future. In fact, if it were absolutely right and utterly sensible, your company would probably already be doing it.[2] It doesn't have to be constructed analytically. The only real requirement is that it be a happy, aspirational story. Your happy story envisions how your organization will win. If the story isn't happy, it isn't worth being an option in the first place.

After happy stories are shared, your group should have developed a robust list of options generated without the stress of these options needing to be logical. This also elevates creativity.[3]

When you have assembled the happy stories and options, then you can ask the most important question in strategy: For each story, what would have to be *true* for it to be a good choice or attractive option? This is the same question as: What will it take for us to succeed?

The group should select the happy story that represents the desired future of the organization. Some of the best attributes of several stories may need to be combined. Once the final happy story is shaped, a final question will be asked: For our selected story, what would it take to *fail*?

Once failure points are noted, goals could then be developed (see the Fail-Succeed technique). Your strategic planning teams may find great inspiration and value in this low-key, creative frame of mind. It can be fun to shape happy stories in smaller teams, and then compare attributes of each story in a larger group, piecing together the best features and then embarking on the more difficult work to determine what must be accomplished to arrive at this happy destination.

Values in Action

The VIA Institute of Character (https://www.viacharacter.org) is an organization focused on helping people discover their character strengths. These six core virtues can be explored for organizations as well as employees: courage, justice, humanity, temperance, transcendence, and wisdom. Based on an analysis offered pre-workshop, the facilitator could ask the questions: What values are you leaning into? How do they support you? How are they getting in the way? How are they creating distractions or pain?

War Rooms and Big Rooms

War rooms have been used in government emergency situations for many years when battle plans were formulated. They were designed for complex and uncertain situations where specific groups of people are called together in a decision-making environment. Today, war rooms (sometimes also called "big rooms") are focused on large, long-term projects. Multiple sources of data are processed and a range of potential decisions filtered in one room or within a dedicated workspace. Personnel, equipment, and materials are located in that specific location.

The core principle for a strategy war room is that it must be set up so present and future scenarios can be seen simultaneously.[4] These rooms feature places to convene and technology that allows critical information to be shared freely without interruption.[5] Those in the room are viewing real-time data alongside developing action and strategies that impact the present and the future. For strategic planning, the dedicated war room would feature wall space where scenario-planning and other activities can be mapped out and saved for further discussions and changes, which fosters group cohesiveness, teamwork, and productivity. War rooms can be set up to uniquely support urgent projects and tasks within a fixed time, often under difficult emergency circumstances such as the COVID-19 global pandemic of 2020.

During the COVID-19 crisis, organizations across the globe were thrown into a situation in which they immediately needed to revise strategic plans in order to survive an unpredictable downturn.

Many business and government organizations set up COVID-19 war rooms. These technology-enabled spaces included both virtual and in-person teams comprised of senior leaders from disciplines including sales, operations, HR, and finance. Interdisciplinary leadership teams examined revenue and cash scenarios—including extreme downside situations. Leaders translated the scenarios into a range of potential revenue declines. They stress-tested profit and loss statements and balance sheets.[6]

Big rooms are created for large-scale projects requiring a variety of perspectives. A design-build firm used the big room concept for hospital updating and construction. The big room became the central planning location for architects, engineers, physicians, and construction management throughout the entire hospital construction process. The team reviewed building designs simulating real life, using 3D technology that turned the space into a virtual hospital. With big-room technology, doctors provided design recommendations from the lobby and complex operating rooms to research laboratories.

Physical war and big rooms can build shared understanding and can help your team work better together when they see decisions being summarized and posted on walls that become living pages. In essence, the room *becomes* the page with whiteboards and empty walls for note taking and storyboarding.[7]

The goal of big room planning is to teach leaders and their organizations how to be more collaborative with customers and respond faster to market needs and pressures.[8] When people are planning within their teams and planning and coordinating with other teams, it gives everyone an overview of what everyone else is doing and the understanding of who is dependent on whom.[9]

Virtual war and big rooms require technology that enables teams to quickly get up to speed on what's known and what's been done, as well as to formulate, execute, and track action plans. Video enhances communication through visual body language. Virtual war rooms also use technology that allows documents, images, and other vital information to be uploaded and shared. The technology enables real-time communication from connected devices and maintains a record of that communication.

Virtual rooms feature one or more large TV monitors, webcams, microphones with noise and echo filters, and a dedicated teleconference or videoconference line or room where information can be centralized and updated in real time. The room needs a shared wiki, virtual document, or whiteboard area where people can view and track the plan. The virtual war room also needs an active chat room or instant message service where side conversation can occur without disrupting the main chatter.[10]

REFERENCES

1. Alight Solutions (2018). Workforce Mindset® Study. https://alight.com/research-insights/tag/alight-research.

2. Amazon (2019). "What is Cloud Computing?" Amazon Web Services. https://aws.amazon.com/what-is-cloud-computing.

3. American Planning Association (2019). Scenario Planning KnowledgeBase. www.planning.org/knowledgebase/scenarioplanning.

4. Apple Inc. (2018). Form 10-K filed with the United States Securities and Exchange Commission.

5. Argenti Strategic Planning (2020). "The Argenti System of Strategic Planning." https://www.argentisys.com/the-system.

6. Association for Strategic Planning (2020a). The Body of Knowledge for Level II Certification, Strategic Management Professional. https://www.strategyassociation.org/page/CertFramework.

7. Association for Strategic Planning (2020b). "Virtual Strategic Plan Development During COVID-19: Coming Together as a Community." Webinar, April 17.

8. Barry, Bryan W. (1997). *Strategic Planning Workbook for Nonprofit Organizations*. Saint Paul, NM: Fieldstone Alliance.

9. Barry, Bryan W. (1998). "A Beginner's Guide to Strategic Planning." *The Futurist* (April): 33–36.

10. Bauer, John (2017). *How To Achieve Your Preferred Future by Answering Ten Critical Questions.* E-book. Location: John E. Bauer Consulting, LLC., Milwaukee, WI.

11. Bergholz, Harvey (2018). "4 Ways to Keep Strategic Planning Focused." Wisconsin School of Business, Center for Professional and Executive Development. https://blog.uwcped.org/4-ways-to-keep-strategic-planning-focused.

12. Bradley, Tony (2016). "Big Room Planning: Getting Everyone on the Same Page." https://devops.com/devops-works-best-when-everyone-is-on-the-same-page.

13. Brown, Brené (2018). "Leading from Hurt Versus Leading from Heart." In *Dare to Lead: Brave Work, Tough Conversations, Whole Hearts.* New York: Random House.

14. Bryson, John M. (2018). *Strategic Planning for Public and Nonprofit Organizations: A Guide to Strengthening and Sustaining Organizational Achievement.* San Francisco: Jossey-Bass.

15. Business Models Inc. (2020). "Set Up a Container for Strategy Discussion: Strategy War Room." https://www.businessmodelsinc.com/war-room.

16. Cars.com (2020). "Our Values." https://www.cars.com/careers.

17. Cherry, Baylor (2019). "18 Captivating Mission Statement Examples You Need to Read." September 20. https://www.bluleadz.com/blog/15-of-the-very-best-mission-statement-examples.

18. ClearPoint Strategy (2020). "Measurement and Tracking System Information and Case Study." https://archive.clearpointstrategy.com/strategic-planning-software.

19. Collins, Jim (2001). *Good to Great: Why Some Companies Make the Leap . . . and Others Don't.* New York: Harper Business.

20. Collins, Jim (2005). *Good to Great and the Social Sectors: Why Business Thinking Is Not the Answer.* New York: Harper Business.

21. Cothran, Henry and Rodney, Clouser (2009 [2006]). *Strategic Planning for Communities, Non-Profit Organizations and Public Agencies.* Gainesville: University of Florida Food and Resource Economics Department, Florida Cooperative Extension Service, Institute of Food and Agricultural Sciences.

22. De Morree, Pim (2020). "A Radical New Vision of the Future of Work." https://www.iabc.com/radical-new-vision-of-work.

23. Emmer, Marc (2017). *Momentum: How Companies Decide What to Do Next.* Valencia, CA: Optimize Inc.

24. Gallup Employee Engagement Report (2018). https://news.gallup.com/poll/241649/employee-engagement-rise.aspx.

25. Ganz, Marshall (2020). "Telling Your Public Story: Self, Us, Now." https://www.welcomingrefugees.org/sites/default/files/documents/resources/Public%20Story%20Worksheet07Ganz.pdf.

26. Gilbert, Rick (2019). "PowerSpeaking Inc." https://www.td.org/magazines/td-magazine/four-presentation-strategies-for-a-c-level-audience.

27. Hansen, Randall S. (2017). "The Five-Step Plan for Creating Personal Mission Statements." December 15. https://www.livecareer.com/quintessential/creating-personal-mission-statements.

28. Heinila, Roope (2020). "Company Values Definition, Importance and Examples." April 23. https://blog.smarp.com/the-importance-of-company-values.

29. Ibarra, Herminia (2015). *Act Like a Leader, Think Like a Leader.* Boston: Harvard Business Review Press.

30. Jepsen, Ole (2020). "Scaling Agile: Big Room Planning." https://www.infoq.com/articles/making-scaling-agile-work-4.

31. Kanter, Rosabeth Moss (2020). *Think Outside the Building: How Advanced Leaders Can Change the World One Smart Innovation at a Time.* New York: Public Affairs | Hachette Book Group.

32. Kaplan, Robert S. and David P. Norton (1992). "The Balanced Scorecard: Measures that Drive Performance." *Harvard Business Review* (January–February), 71–79.

33. Kaplan, Robert S. and David P. Norton (2001). *The Strategy-Focused Organization.* Boston: Harvard Business School Press.

34. Kath, Carla (2020). "3 Ways to Unleash Your Internal Influencers to Produce Results." https://staffbase.com/blog/3-ways-to-unleash-your-internal-influencers-to-produce-results.

35. Kijko, Paweł (2017). "The War Room Concept in Project Management." https://www.timecamp.com/blog/2017/01/the-war-room-concept-in-project-management.

36. Kim, W. Chan and Renée Mauborgne (2015). *Blue Ocean Strategy: How to Create Uncontested Market Space and Make the Competition Irrelevant.* Boston: Harvard Business School Publishing.

37. Knapp, Jake (2014). "Why Your Team Needs a War Room—and How to Set One Up." June 10. https://library.gv.com/why-your-team-needs-a-war-room-and-how-to-set-one-up-498e940e3487.

38. Kono, Pedro M. and Barry Barnes (2010). "The Role of Finance in the Strategic-Planning and Decision-Making Process." *Graziadio Business Review* 13, no. 1. https://gbr.pepperdine.edu/2010/08/the-role-of-finance-in-the-strategic-planning-and-decision-making-process.

39. Kotter, John P. (1995). "Leading Change: Why Transformation Efforts Fail." *Harvard Business Review* (March–April): 59–67.

40. Kusibab, Stephanie (2019). "Essentials for Virtual Meetings: Keeping Everyone Engaged and Contributing." https://www.essentiamstrategy.com/essentials-for-virtual-meetings.

41. LaPiana Consulting (2019). "Principles for Strategy Management." May 2. https://www.lapiana.org/insights-for-the-sector/insights/strategic-planning/principles-for-strategy-development.

42. LaPiana, David (2008). *The Nonprofit Strategy Revolution: Real-Time Strategic Planning in a Rapid-Response World.* New York: Fieldstone Alliance.

43. Levie, Aaron (2020). "Interview with Box CEO Aaron Levie." https://www.linkedin.com/video/live/urn:li:ugcPost:6669266443806281729.

44. Levine, Stuart R. (2017). "Why Your Strategic Plan Will Never Succeed." *Forbes Magazine*, April 25. https://www.forbes.com/sites/forbesinsights/2017/04/25/why-your-strategic-plan-will-never-succeed/#45a566264f74.

45. Liberating Structures (2020). "1-2-4-All." http://www.liberatingstructures.com/1-1-2-4-all.

46. Lynch, Cecilia (2019). "How to Hire Your Next Strategic Planning Consultant." https://www.focusedmomentum.com/blog/how-to-hire-a-strategic-planning-consultant.

47. McKinsey (2007). "How To Improve Strategic Planning." https:// www.mckinsey.com/business-functions/strategy-and-corporate-finance/ our-insights/how-to-improve-strategic-planning.

48. McKinsey (2020). "Making Game Theory Work for Managers." https:// www.mckinsey.com/business-functions/strategy-and-corporate-finance/ our-insights/making-game-theory-work-for-managers.

49. McNeilly, Mark (2014). "How to Avoid a 'Strategy Fail'." *Fast Company* Magazine, February 14. https://www.fastcompany.com/3025681/ how-to-avoid-a-strategy-fail.

50. Mintzberg, Henry (1978). "Patterns in Strategy Formation." *Management Science* 24, no. 9 (May): 934–948.

51. Mintzberg, Henry (1994). *The Rise and Fall of Strategic Planning.* New York: The Free Press.

52. Nink, Marcos (2015). "Many Employees Don't Know What's Expected of Them at Work." *Business Journal*, October 13, https://news.gallup. com/businessjournal/186164/employees-don-know-expected-work. aspx.

53. Poore, Carol A. (2001). *Building Your Career Portfolio.* New York: Cengage.

54. Porter, Michael E. (1980). *Competitive Strategy: Techniques for Analyzing Industries and Competitors.* New York: The Free Press.

55. Porter, Michael E., Jay W. Lorsch, and Nitin Nohria (2004). "Seven Surprises for New CEOs." *Harvard Business Review* (October). https://hbr.org/2004/10/seven-surprises-for-new-ceos.

56. Potter, Les (2009). *The Communication Plan: The Heart of Strategic Communication, 2nd edition.* San Francisco: International Association of Business Communicators.

57. Prezi (2018). "Survey Finds Attention Spans Aren't Shrinking— They're Evolving." August 28, based on the 2018 State of Attention Report. https://www.prnewswire.com/news-releases/survey-finds- attention-spans-arent-shrinking--theyre-evolving-300702833. html#:~:text=More%20effective%20storytelling%20in%20 business,keeps%20them%20engaged%20with%20content.

58. Riel, Jennifer and Roger L. Martin (2017). *Creating Great Choices: A Leader's Guide to Integrative Thinking.* Boston: Harvard Business School Publishing.

59. Robbins, Lisa (2008). "Decision Theater Tests Pandemic Flu Plans." *ASU Now*, May 14, https://asunow.asu.edu/content/decision-theater-tests-pandemic-flu-plans.

60. Robbins, Stephen P., Mary Coulter, and David A. DeCenzo (2017). *Fundamentals of Management.* Boston: Pearson.

61. Rooke, David and William Torgert (2005). "Seven Transformations of Leadership." *Harvard Business Review* 83, no. 4 (April). https://hbr.org/2005/04/seven-transformations-of-leadership.

62. Rowland, Christine (2019). "Apple Inc.'s Mission Statement and Vision Statement (An Analysis)," February 13. Panmore Institute. http://panmore.com/apple-mission-statement-vision-statement.

63. Saenz, Herman and Dunigan O'Keeffe (2020). "Covid-19: Protect, Recover and Retool." https://www.bain.com/insights/covid-19-protect-recover-and-retool.

64. Seeds for Change (2019). "Facilitating Meetings." https://www.seedsforchange.org.uk/facilitationmeeting.

65. Simpplr (2019). "Employee Engagement Survey Linked to Glassdoor Data." https://www.simpplr.com/blog/2019/simpplr-research-employee-engagement-survey-linked-to-glassdoor-data.

66. Small Business & Entrepreneurship Council (2020). "Facts and Data on Small Business and Entrepreneurship." https://sbecouncil.org/about-us/facts-and-data.

67. Target Corporation (2020). "Target Outlines 2020 Strategic Initiatives," March 3. https://corporate.target.com/press/releases/2020/03/target-outlines-2020-strategic-initiatives#:~:text=In%202020%2C%20Target%20will%20enhance,Pickup%20and%20Drive%20Up%20fulfillment.

68. Tayyar, Fayez (2020). "5 Dashboards That Will Boost CEOs' Strategic Decisions." https://corporater.com/en/5-dashboards-that-will-boost-ceos-strategic-decisions.

69. Tearle, Ruth (2019). *Strategy for CEOs: A Step By Step Guide.* George, South Africa: Change Designs Business Books.

70. Tomboc, Kai (2019). "Do I Need an Animated Infographic?" https://www.easel.ly/blog/do-i-need-an-animated-infographic.

71. Weaver, Jenna (2019). "Strategic Planning Software: How To Chart & Track Your Course." https://www.clearpointstrategy.com/strategic-planning-software.

72. Winch, Guy (2013). "10 Signs That You Might Have Fear of Failure." *Psychology Today*, June 18. https://www.psychologytoday.com/us/blog/the-squeaky-wheel/201306/10-signs-you-might-have-fear-failure#:~:text=Rather%2C%20a%20fear%20of%20failure,makes%20them%20feel%20deep%20shame.

73. Wonderflow (2020). "50+ Focus Group Questions to Ask for Valuable Customer Feedback." https://www.wonderflow.co/blog/focus-group-questions.

74. Wu, John (2018). "How Do You Build a War Room for a Virtual Team?" https://www.quora.com/How-do-you-build-a-war-room-for-a-virtual-team.

75. Zomorrodian, Asghar (2017). "New Trends on Strategic Planning: Virtual Environment, Tech Innovation, Globalization & Organizational Performance." Paper presented at 24th Annual Meeting of American Society of Business & Behavioral Sciences, March 25, Las Vegas.

NOTES

PREFACE

1. Small Business & Entrepreneurship Council (2020).

CHAPTER 1

1. A McKinsey survey conducted in late July and early August 2006 received 796 responses from a panel of executives from around the world. All panelists have mostly financial or strategic responsibilities and work in a wide range of industries for organizations with revenues of at least $500 million. Of the executives who responded, 55 percent said they were very dissatisfied with their organization's strategic-planning program, including the planning experience (McKinsey 2007). According to Kaplan and Norton, in 2001, only *7 percent of the workforce understand their company's direction* and what's expected of them (Kaplan and Norton 2001). A second study in 2009 showed that only 14 percent of the polled organizations reported that employees had a good understanding of their company's strategy and direction.

2. Alight Solutions (2018).

3. Zomorrodian (2017).

4. Argenti Strategic Planning (2020).

5. Emmer (2017).

6. Porter, Lorsch, and Nohria (2004).

7. Association for Strategic Planning (2020).

8. Kanter (2020).
9. Mintzberg (1994).
10. Mintzberg (1994).
11. Lynch (2019).

CHAPTER 2

1. Kotter (1995).
2. Target Corporation (2020).
3. LaPiana (2019).
4. Kaplan and Norton (1992).
5. Collins (2001).
6. Porter (1980).
7. McNeilly (2014).
8. American Planning Association (2019).
9. Wonderflow (2020).

CHAPTER 3

1. Simpplr (2019).
2. Barry (1998).
3. Ibarra (2015).
4. Kono and Barnes (2010).
5. Mintzberg (1978).
6. Kim and Mauborgne (2015).
7. Riel and Martin (2017).

CHAPTER 4

1. Levie (2020).
2. Kusibab (2019).
3. Kusibab (2019).
4. McKinsey (2013).

CHAPTER 5

1. Rooke and Torgert (2005).
2. Kelton Global and Prezi (2018).
3. Prezi and Pew Research Center (2018).
4. Prezi and Pew Research Center (2018).
5. Rowland (2019).
6. Apple (2018).
7. Cherry (2019).
8. Mission statement from TED website: https://www.ted.com/about/our-organization#:~:text=Our%20Mission%3A%20Spread%20ideas,and%2C%20ultimately%2C%20the%20world.
9. Heinila (2020).
10. Apple's website: https://investor.apple.com/apple-values/default.aspx.
11. Cars.com website: https://www.cars.com/careers.

CHAPTER 6

1. Kaplan and Norton (1992).
2. Nink (2015).
3. Weaver (2019) and ClearPoint Strategy (2019).
4. Tayyor (2020).
5. ClearPoint Strategy (2020).
6. Amazon (2019).

CHAPTER 7

1. Gallup (2018).
2. De Morree (2020).
3. Levine (2017).
4. Kath (2020).
5. Tomboc (2019).
6. Tomboc (2019).

CHAPTER 8

1. Collins (2001) and (2005).
2. Winch (2013).
3. Poore (2001).
4. Hansen (2017).

APPENDIX

1. Liberating Structures (2020).
2. Riel and Martin (2017).
3. Riel and Martin (2017).
4. Business Models Inc. (2020).
5. Kijko (2017).
6. Saenz and O'Keeffe (2020).
7. Knapp (2014).
8. Bradley (2016).
9. Jepsen (2020).
10. Wu (2018).

ABOUT THE AUTHOR

CAROL A. POORE is president of Poore and Associates Strategic Planning, providing strategic planning expertise for corporate, nonprofit, and social sector executive teams around the world, expanding organizational capacity and strategic impact.

Her vital strategic planning framework has assisted organizations with innovative growth and turnaround, strategic fundraising, venture capital development, storytelling, branding, identity building, and civic engagement.

Carol's executive and strategic planning roles have included serving as president and CEO of a healthcare and clinical trials research center, as vice provost at Arizona State University, as vice president of a medical technology incubator, and as a senior strategist at Salt River Project Water and Power, one of the world's largest public power utilities and suppliers of water based in Phoenix, Arizona.

A faculty member at Arizona State University since 2011, Carol teaches graduate and undergraduate courses in leadership for change, public policy, and community development. Her extensive board leadership as well as her heart for community service and philanthropy spans hospital and healthcare, bank, municipal, university, and nonprofit social services, economic development, and arts/culture organizations. Author of *Building Your Career Portfolio* (Cengage), Carol provides inspirational keynotes and professional development workshops, webinars, articles, and interviews focused on leading with purpose and strategic impact.

Carol received her Ph.D. in public administration, her MBA, and her bachelor of science degree in journalism and broadcasting from Arizona State University. Her research focuses on social capital and its connection to vibrant community development and downtown revitalization. For more information, visit CarolPoore.com as well as LinkedIn.

Safety + trust
respect history but not bound by old ways
Creating the future we want
state unstated assumptions

proactive comms
clarity on ownership

Made in the USA
Coppell, TX
02 November 2021